BARGELLO MAGIC

by PAULINE FISCHER and ANABEL LASKER

BARGELLO MAGIC

How to design your own

Holt, Rinehart and Winston

NEW YORK   CHICAGO   SAN FRANCISCO

Acknowledgments

With thanks to my daughter Claire Kahane, to Renee Lipson, to my friends Lena Teitelbaum and Gertrude Golding who worked some Bargello samples from my designs.

My sincere appreciation to the curators of the textile divisions of the Victoria and Albert Museum, London, the Museo Nazionale, Florence, and the Musée des Arts Decoratifs, Paris, for allowing me to use their facilities for my research.

And very special thanks to Mrs. Muriel Bishop, the teachers' teacher, and to Linda Ormesson of the Embroiderers' Guild.

P.F.

Sincere appreciation to Karen Mender, Joan Pryor, Ella Projansky, and Rene Richman for valuable assistance in working designs.

Gratitude to Rosetta Larson and Dorothy Perkins for assistance in selecting materials.

Grateful thanks to Catherine Hedlund, William Justema, Jean Mailey, and Erica Wilson for their courses in needlework and design, and to Miss Elisabeth Hall, curator of the N.Y. Horticultural Society Library, for her assistance in my research.

A.L.

We are deeply indebted to Pace Barnes, the editor who made *Bargello Magic* possible, and to Betty Binns, the designer who shaped it into a coherent whole.

P.F. and A.L.

Published simultaneously in Canada by Holt, Rinehart and Winston of Canada, Limited.

ISBN: 0-03-088259-1
Library of Congress Catalog Card Number: 79-182757

Published, November 1972
Fourth Printing, December 1973

Designer: Betty Binns
Printed in the United States of America: 039

*To my grandchildren Danielle, Peter, Madeleine,
and Suzanne and to my numerous students whose original
ideas inspired me to write this book.*

P.F.

*To my sons and the children of my workshop program at the
Botanical Garden for whom I wrote the anatomy of creativity,
the language of design.*

A.L.

Contents

Preface

Bargello is a type of embroidery which has become fused with Florentine, Flame, Hungarian Point, Brick, and Byzantine stitches. In the United States, the word Bargello has become the family name for all these upright stitches. Easy to master and economical to use, Bargello can be adapted to an unlimited number of patterns worked on canvas and is an ideal medium for learning about design.

Bargello Magic will teach you how to design your own patterns through careful selection of colors and materials. Beginning with the basics of selecting needle, yarn, and canvas, you will learn to work with other textures such as cotton, silk, and metallic threads—even twine and human hair.

"Starting on the Right Track" should be read by beginning and experienced needleworkers alike, for it is here that hints are given on where to start and what to avoid.

The heart of *Bargello Magic* is the second section, "Principles of Design and Their Application." The "Language of Design" is a practical course in learning the vocabulary of good design and applying it to your own experience. You will learn how to vary patterns, how to create new designs and repeats, how to adapt drawings and paintings, and how to create custom textiles for your interiors. Included are 10 variations of a single pattern to demonstrate the remarkable interplay of color on design.

In the "Notebook of Patterns," more than 50 designs for overall patterns are shown in full color, along with diagrams of selected complicated areas, hints on color or material substitutions, and occasional suggestions for projects. The patterns range from traditional to modern and include such diverse styles as Oriental, English, French, Pennsylvania Dutch, and Op Art.

In the Notebook, patterns have been placed in sequence according to difficulty and are numbered for easy reference since they are occasionally cited in other chapters. The names are part whimsy, part history, part grateful acknowledgment to Elsa Williams who introduced Bargello to the vocabulary of American needlewomen with her outstanding first book of Bargello patterns. In grading the patterns, we have tried to place them in order of complexity of stitch and color combinations. There is some overlapping in their placement—a subjective view at best—but you will be well advised to practice before starting on the difficult ones.

A separate section is included on borders, for which Bargello is especially suited.

Often patterns on facing pages are related and their stitch direction or color variations should be studied together. Sometimes Bargello is depicted with needlepoint or canvas stitches. We have not attempted to diagram or explain them since stitchery is beyond the scope of this book. In "Sources of Information" you will find a selected list, organized under subject, that suggests books on stitch techniques, projects, and other areas of needlework not dealt with here.

All patterns in this book are worked on 16-mesh canvas unless otherwise noted.

Bargello Magic is an invitation to explore the basic elements and principles of design. Learn how to put them to work to create new patterns especially suited to your personal needs.

MATERIALS AND TECHNIQUES

Easy access to relatively few, inexpensive materials and the re-discovery of an age-old, versatile quick stitch are two important reasons for the popularity of needlework in the 1970s. Art needlework shops abound and larger stores from dime stores to department stores have introduced sections featuring everything from designer kits to raw materials for your own creations.

Bargello needlepoint is a compact craft. Its materials can be carried in a pocketbook or a tote bag. But whether making a coaster or a couch cover, the materials are the same—a piece of canvas, enough yarn to cover it, a needle to sew with, and scissors to cut and correct. Your pattern may be simple or complex, but once you have mastered the pattern repeats, the design goes with you.

Designing your own needlework is what this book is about. Understanding what the materials are and how to use them is the first stage to success. You will find the basic tools nearby, either at a local needlework shop or by mail order,* and armed with a good knowledge of the techniques of Bargello, you will be ready to do your own projects.

CANVAS

Canvas is the fabric generally used to work Bargello patterns. It is a coarse material, evenly woven, and usually made of cotton

* In a few cases we recommend items by brand names that may not be readily available; for information on where to write see "Sources of Information."

Bargello materials

which has been stiffened with sizing to hold its shape. (Finer-mesh canvas is also made of linen, but it is more expensive than cotton canvas and is not always available. Linen canvas has a long life because its highly polished threads accept harder wear and tear.) Canvas is sold by the yard and is made in widths ranging from 18 to 60 inches. Canvas should be firm, without knots, and have threads of even thickness. It comes in various sizes which are determined by the number of meshes or "holes" per inch, and its color may be white, ecru, or antique. The color of the canvas may affect the finished appearance of a design. Select ecru or antique for dark or muted patterns. White canvas is necessary for those which employ white or light-colored wools.

The texture of a finished piece of Bargello is influenced greatly by the coarseness of the canvas. Jewel boxes and bags requiring delicate mountings should be worked on fine-mesh canvas. Rugs and wall hangings can be worked on grosser canvas weaves. The number of meshes to an inch determines the coarseness of the canvas, and the smaller number of stitches to an inch, the coarser the canvas will be.

Bargello patterns are keyed to counting meshes or threads, and care should be taken to select canvas that is easy on your eyesight. Canvas sizes range from the large with 3 to 5 meshes per inch, used for rugs, to the fine gauze available up to 40 meshes per inch. For pillows, samplers, and chair seats, 14 to 16 meshes per inch are preferred; 18-mesh canvas is suitable for handbags, eyeglass cases, and belts. *All patterns in this book are worked on size 16 canvas unless otherwise specified.*

Canvas is available in two weaves: single thread (mono) and double thread (Penelope).

Mono-canvas This canvas has single, evenly spaced warp and woof threads,* and is preferred for Bargello because of the ease in counting single threads and the uniformity of spaces for stitch repeats and pattern transfers.

Mono-canvas comes in widths of 18, 36, 40, 54, and 60 inches and in mesh sizes of 10, 12, 14, 16, 18, 24, and 28.

Penelope canvas This canvas has double threads for each mesh. With doubling, however, the threads are unequally spaced, and for Bargello work, it is more difficult to cover the canvas evenly. Penelope canvas is slower to work because care must be taken to avoid fraying the yarn as it passes through the small meshes, and in Bargello stitchery, the double threads must be separated as you work each stitch. This canvas is less apt to stretch, its threads are thinner, and it is stronger than mono. There is an advantage to using Penelope canvas when combining Bargello with crewel and needlepoint. By working between the double threads extra stitches can be added to develop intricate patterns. The extra threads are also helpful in working shadings, shadows, for spacing initials, and in picking up extra meshes for composite Bargello patterns.

Penelope canvas comes in widths of 18, 36, 40, and 60 inches, and in mesh sizes of 3, 4, 5, 7, 8, 9, 10, and 12 per inch.

Rug canvas Stronger canvas made of hard, twisted cotton threads, distinguished by larger meshes is available in both mono-canvas and Penelope.

Mono rug canvas has single threads and working on it causes less eyestrain. For Bargello rugs, we recommend 10- to 12-mesh canvas. It comes in widths of 36, 40, and 54 inches and is available in needlework departments or on special order.

Penelope rug canvas, like Penelope embroidery canvas, has double threads for each mesh. These paired woof and warp threads make this material excellent for rugs because Penelope holds its shape better than mono, allows for pattern development in extra meshes, and is easier to join when worked in sections. It comes in 40-inch widths and may be ordered in 72-inch widths. The meshes range from 3½ and 4, to 5 per inch.

---

* Warp threads are the vertical or upright threads in a canvas. The horizontal threads passed between these warp threads in the weaving process are known as woof threads.

Other "canvas" Almost any even-weave fabric can be substituted for canvas in working Bargello patterns. *Lauder linen gauze* and open-weave linens are particularly adaptable. Care should be taken to select materials which have even thread rows and are free of knots. *Hardanger cloth* and *monk's cloth* have threads woven in pairs and they should be worked in one direction only since the warp and woof threads are not of the same thickness. These materials are sold by the yard in fabric shops.

Whatever you use, be sure to select fabrics in which the threads in the weave are easily distinguishable. Avoid canvas or fabrics abrasive to the touch as they may fray the threads. Synthetic canvas, though less expensive, is stiff and very abrasive. If the canvas is colored, wet a swatch thoroughly to check if it is colorfast.

YARNS AND THREADS

Wool yarn is preferred for Bargello and today it is both colorfast and mothproof. Wool yarns differ in weight, in number of plies (strands), and in the way these plies are twisted to form the yarn. Because the canvas must be covered, the type of yarns or threads selected depends on the size of the mesh. If the thread is too heavy for the canvas, it will push the mesh out of place and the finished piece will be puckered; if the yarn is too thin, the canvas threads will not be covered. The coarser the canvas, the fewer the meshes per square inch, so that the yarn should be thicker than that used for finer-mesh canvas. You must also consider how the finished piece will be used when selecting yarns and threads. Silk, mercerized cotton, and metallic threads are not as durable as wool. A footstool, or rug receiving constant wear should be worked with threads that are coarser and more serviceable than the threads and yarns used for dainty accent pillows.

Wool yarns adaptable to Bargello are discussed below.

Persian yarn This is a 2-ply wool available in 3-thread strands which can be worked singly or together. (Because Bargello may require additional threads to cover the meshes, wool available in 3 strands allows you to split the yarn and increase the number of strands used.) The extensive color range of Persian yarn offers great opportunity for color combinations. Paternayan wool is the finest Persian yarn made in the United States because of its long fibers, 3-thread strand, and wide color range. The colors are vibrant, and full of sheen. Since color gradation is very important in Bargello, the numbered and graded color charts available from wool suppliers are useful in making color selections. Sold by the ounce or skein, and available at needlework stores, Persian yarn is the most versatile material for canvas work because it can be used in a wide range of meshes.

Tapestry yarn This is a 4-ply wool twisted into one strand which makes it impractical for splitting. It is excellent for No. 10 or 12 canvas if care is taken to avoid uneven stitches caused by twisting of threads when doubled. Tapestry yarn may vary in twist according to the manufacturer. It is available in 8.8 and 40-yard skeins in many colors including muted tints and shades. Frequently used in needlepoint kits, it has a tendency to fluff up and wear thin if worked with too long a thread.

Crewel yarn This is a fine, 2-ply wool used for crewel embroidery. Adaptable to fine-mesh canvas if the proper number of strands is used, it comes in a wide range of colors. If care is taken to keep the threads from twisting there is no reason why crewel yarn cannot be combined with tapestry yarn. Crewel yarn is available at needlework shops and is sold by the pound or in skeins.

Knitting yarn This is 4-ply wool, less expensive than tapestry or Persian wools, available in a large selection of colors at most needlework shops. Used doubled, it will cover larger meshes. Stitch tension must be regulated with this wool since it is elastic and tends to pull the canvas out of shape. It also has a tendency to fluff and mat into a tangle, and is not as durable as the yarns made especially for needlework.

Rug yarn Paternayan rug yarn has a 2-ply, 3-thread strand and is available in a multitude of colors in 4-ounce or 1-pound skeins. Another rug yarn, Colbert, is spun and dyed in France by Les Filatures de St. Epin, under the name of Laines du Bon Pasteur. D.M.C. rug yarns are available in a wide variety of colors.

Yarn for allergic stitchers A cotton yarn made by D.M.C. under the name of Retors à Broder is available for stitchers allergic to wool. It comes in a lovely range of colors in skeins of 11 yards each. It is washable, colorfast, and suitable for No. 10 or 12 canvas.

D.M.C. Mouliné This is a 6-strand floss mercerized cotton with a large range of colors available at needlework stores in skeins of 27 yards. It adds interest and highlights to a design especially when used next to yarns. It is not as durable as wool but is excellent for textural contrast, though it is not recommended if subject to hard wear. Because it is generally used in small quantities as a highlight, its placement can be planned for minimum abrasive wear. Having less elasticity than silk, it is easier to work, though you must watch that your stitches lie evenly side by side.

Silk thread This is a delightful medium for the experienced needlewoman. It produces a luminosity that lends highlights, and when used in moderation, gives accent to important areas of a composition. It is expensive, not recommended for hard wear, and because of its sheen, should be used with restraint. Sold by the skein, it may have to be specially ordered. Pearsalls Filo Floss, a 6-strand silk thread, is our preference.

Rayon thread   This gives a similar effect to that of silk and is less expensive, easier to work with, and is available in skeins or balls. Ask your dealer for Marlitt or Bella Donna threads.

Metallic thread   This thread is more difficult to use than other types of thread because of its construction. Metallic threads usually consist of an outer metallic casing wrapped around an inner core of silk, cotton, or nylon. The outer casing may separate with continuous exposure to canvas mesh, and short lengths should be used to minimize fraying. Though many types of metallic thread can be found, we recommend Lamé. Available in silver and gold on spools, its casing is made of metallic-colored plastic which will not tarnish. So-called "silver" threads made of aluminum will not tarnish either. Metallic threads must be doubled (sometimes tripled) to cover the

TABLE 1
**Number of strands and types of yarns
suitable for different mesh sizes**

Type of wool	Number of meshes in canvas per inch	Bargello strands	Needlepoint strands
Persian yarn	10	5–6	3
	12	4–5	2–3
	14	3	2
	16	3	1–2
	18	2	1
Tapestry yarn	10	2	1
	12	2	1
	14	1	
Crewel	Test on canvas		
Knitting	Test on canvas		

canvas, so buy extra thread from single dye lots. These threads are available in gold, silver, copper, and pewter tones.

Selection of yarns and threads

Manufacturers have different specifications for contour, thickness, twists, and substances. Their yarns vary accordingly. The preceding table suggests the number of strands and types of yarns suitable for different meshes. Since different patterns require more threads to cover longer stitches it is recommended that several repeats of your pattern be first worked on a doodle canvas before a final decision is made as to the number of strands.

COMBINING YARNS AND THREADS WITH OTHER MATERIALS

Combining other materials with embroidery wools will lend variety to your work. Mercerized crochet cotton, linen threads, string, raffia, or even human hair can give interesting textures to a Bargello pattern. Hair work known also as Point Tresse was an art craft of the Middle Ages. In India the hair of the elephant's tail was plaited into a thread for weaving or sewing. In England unusual effects were obtained in embroidery with the use of human hair, particularly silver white hair, which was twisted before sewing around a fine silver or linen thread. In America, the Victorians sewed the hair from their combings into flowers, leaves, and sprays. In addition, ends cut from fabric looms when weaving is finished (known as thrums) offer textural variety.

NEEDLES

Tapestry needles with blunt ends and elongated eyes are used for canvas work. The best needles are made of English steel and vary in size from the smallest, size 24, to the largest, size 13. Bargello stitches require larger needles than other needlework because the stitches are longer and more strands of wool are required to cover the meshes. The size of the needle's eye is important, for it must receive the yarn without fraying or twisting its threads. The needle itself should not be too wide to cause stress as it pulls and pushes against the canvas meshes. It should pass through the mesh without stretching it, making a hole in the canvas just large enough for the wool to work in and cover the canvas.

Needles should be discarded if they have become worn from rubbing against the canvas; wool will catch on the top of the worn needle causing the wool to fray and the canvas to shred. There may be a chemical reaction from excessive acid in the fingers, turning the needle dark. Discard this needle be-

TABLE 2

Needle numbers for Persian yarn, metallic or silk thread suitable for different canvas mesh sizes

| Canvas number | Tapestry needle number * | |
	For Persian yarn	For metallic and silk thread †
10	18	18
12	18	18
14	19	18
16	19	18
18	21	18–20 (depending on texture of thread)

* Needle sizes vary according to manufacturer; these specifications are for needles made by W. Crowley and Sons.

† The most suitable needle for metallic and silk threads is a No. 18 because these threads are fragile and the larger eye receives these delicate threads with a minimum of fraying.

cause it will no longer slide easily through the canvas, or polish
it with an emery bag. Run your needles through an emery bag
occasionally to keep them clean. They should be kept in
needle cases made of felt, empty pill bottles, or corks.

Needles are packaged in uniform sizes and it is a good idea
to have extra ones in the proper size at hand.

Table 2 will help you make proper needle choices.

SCISSORS

Missed stitches are a hazard in Bargello and correcting mistakes
early is a must. You will need a special pair of scissors, preferably small, pointed ones that you use only for sewing your
needlework. For fast ripping, insert a sharp scissor point between the canvas and the thread loops and cut the loops,
taking care not to cut the canvas. Then take a pair of tweezers
and pull out the threads. This will cause a minimum of stretching to the canvas. Seam rippers are available, but should be
used with great caution.

A second, larger pair of scissors is needed specifically for
cutting canvas; do not use your sewing scissors since the
coarse grain of the canvas will dull the cutting edges.

MISCELLANEOUS AIDS

Thimble Although optional, a thimble is recommended, for it
is useful in guiding the needle through the canvas mesh, and it
will protect your finger from abrasion. Select a thimble that fits
snugly to ensure even pressure in pushing the needle rhythmi-
cally in and out of the canvas. Ornate thimbles should be
avoided because of their limited working surfaces.

Measuring tape and ruler A measuring tape is needed for
placing the design on the canvas and for checking the design

repeat. A steel measuring tape is accurate, easy to carry, and does not curl or fade like the more commonly used cloth tapes. Small, plastic sewing rulers are also available and are very handy for work on fine-mesh canvas.

Hat pin A hat pin is an asset to check your pattern for errors or to find the next sequence of stitches in the design. Do not use a lead pencil to tick off the stitches because it may mark the yarn.

Beeswax If you use metallic or silk threads, rub them with beeswax after the needle is threaded to keep the ends from fraying. (The excessive wax can be removed later by pressing the finished piece with a warm iron between clean, absorbent surfaces.) Beeswax is available in blocks at notions counters or hardware stores.

Masking tape This self-adhesive tape is ideal for protecting surfaces, and in needlework it is used to bind raw canvas edges, to mount canvas on stretchers, and to cover the rough edges of blocking boards. Tape for canvas edges should be 1- or 1½-inches wide. It is available in rolls at art supply, hardware, and stationery stores.

Marking pens All needlework designs require some marking on the canvas, whether it be for the simple margins of a Bargello geometric or an intricate needlepoint painting. Whatever medium you use, it must be waterproof. Illustrator's waterproof India Ink ballpens are useful to outline your border, establish margins, mark centers, or for any straight-line drawing. Use India Ink with pen or brush to place an outline on canvas. A Sharpie pen is excellent for drawing designs or

repeats, and a Dri-Mark pen is best for coloring your design. (If you use a colored marking pen make certain that colors will not run, and that the color you use is lighter than the yarn that covers it.)

Graph paper Experimenting on paper is the best way to begin a new design. Here you can create your own patterns and observe the effect of color substitutions on established designs. Graph paper is obtainable in a variety of scales and grids equal to some canvas meshes in transparent or opaque sheets at art supply stores.

Frames The frames used for needlework range from hoops, sewing bird clamps, and scroll rods to rotating frames. For Bargello, however, a frame is not necessary unless you are using fine-mesh canvas, working a piece with horizontal and vertical lines, or doing a sampler using a variety of stitches (which tend to pull the canvas out of shape). Artist's stretchers such as those used for oil paintings make ideal frames to solve these problems of changing tensions and allow you to free both hands to shape stitches. Select a frame with the inside measurements equal to the size of your piece of canvas including borders and upholstery allowances. For example, a pillow with a 14-inch finished size requires a frame with an outside measurement of 21 inches. These stretchers, available in a variety of sizes at art supply stores, come in sections ready to assemble.

Tote bags Containers for your needlework come in all sizes and shapes and can be made with pockets and flaps for scissors, ruler, yarns, and thimbles. When you have several projects going at once, plastic bags are ideal for keeping wools separate and for preventing them from becoming dusty or soiled.

The name Bargello has become popular in recent years because it represents a fast technique of stitchery that has attracted the novice and experienced alike. Simple to comprehend and quick to work, its results can be both stunning and satisfying.

Since it is not necessary to purchase predesigned canvas for this stitchery, Bargello has stimulated a renaissance of original design, some good and some bad. The variety of stitches and color combinations provide unlimited possibilities for creating and adapting patterns, and it is essential that you learn how basic patterns are developed before branching out on your own.

Principles of Bargello

Bargello incorporates a number of different though related stitches which have common characteristics. They (1) are parallel to the canvas threads; (2) are usually worked over the same number of threads; (3) frequently overlap in adjoining rows; (4) develop into geometric patterns which are set by the initial row of stitches; and (5) often employ a wide variety of subtle color changes.

To understand how Bargello patterns develop, it is important to see their structure. The following stitch combinations illustrate the principles of Bargello and will enable you to vary your patterns.

Bargello techniques

Stitch over thread or threads in even rows Figure 1a shows stitches covering 2, 3, 4, 5, and 6 threads worked vertically. Varying the number of threads * a stitch covers will change the pattern. Stitches may also be worked horizontally as in Figure 1b or diagonally.

Step In Figures 2a–d adjoining stitches "step" up over different numbers of threads. They are coded as to step and thread count as follows: step count follows thread count separated by a dot. Therefore 2.1 indicates that each stitch is over 2 threads and steps up 1 thread per column; 3.2 means each stitch is over 3 threads and steps up 2; 4.2 is over 4, up 2; and 8.2 is over 8 up 2.

Step up or down Figure 3a illustrates a step pattern of 2.1 in which the step moves upward three columns before starting downward to complete the uniform pattern. The direction changes in Figure 3b as the step increases from 1 to 2 at points marked X. Learn to watch patterns for these changes in step and direction.

Stitches in pairs or blocks In Figure 4a note that the stitches are in pairs and blocks. These groups often vary in pattern sequence (Fig. 4b), providing thicks and thins that must be controlled for effective design.†

Interval with repeat An open sawtooth mesh is created when the repeat is delayed by "rounding" the peak as in Figure 5 (see points marked X for step variation). The next row of stitches fits into these meshes and if a contrasting color is used, the "teeth" will be prominent. Interlocking stitches are the basis for the Brick Stitch frequently used for background fillers.

* You may prefer to count meshes instead of threads.

† There is no shorthand for paired blocks. The formula used on pattern graphs applies only to the number of threads the yarn covers and the thread count of the steps. Since blocks of stitches vary greatly in some patterns, the formulas for block changes would be incomprehensible.

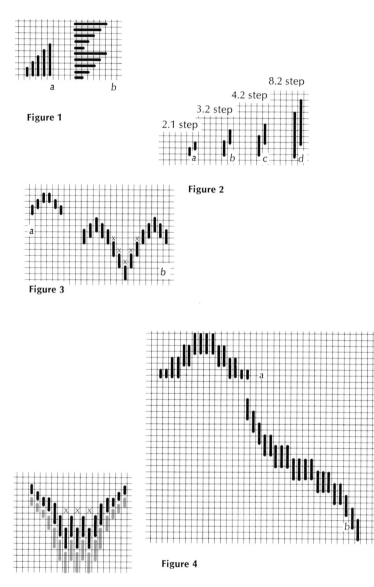

Figure 1

Figure 2

Figure 3

Figure 4

Figure 5

Voids In some patterns an open column or mesh is left between stitch sequences. In Figure 6 you can see that the open space between the "branches" of the tree is allotted to the "trunk" of the row above; similarly, the combination of stitches that form the trunk repeat creates space for the "branches" of the row below. Voids may be filled with background color, may be the beginning of a secondary pattern, or may provide space for the repeat.

Sharing a mesh To completely cover the canvas in Bargello the bottom of the stitch in the row above shares a mesh with the top of the stitch in the row below. This ensures a uniform coverage of the canvas meshes.

Meshes may also be shared in a change of direction. Stitches share meshes perpendicularly in Figure 7a. In Figure 7b, where the steps are inverted to shape an enclosed form, the vertical stitches join at the points marked X in a shared mesh. The direction of the stitches and steps may change after sharing a mesh. Mesh sharing is often used to create forms, and if your pattern count is off, check to see whether the pattern indicates shared meshes for they are easily missed.

Scale and proportion variations Design developments can be evolved by changing the length of the stitches, by doubling the repeats of the stitches, or by increasing the number of stitches between interval repeats. Figures 8a and b illustrate methods of changing scale and proportion in established designs.

Compensation stitches When patterns are worked on the diagonal or when the pattern track is not completed at the border, compensation stitches will be needed to finish the canvas. These are half or partial stitches that result when patterns become fragmented. Other uses for compensation stitches include fitting backgrounds against central motifs, filling voids, etc.

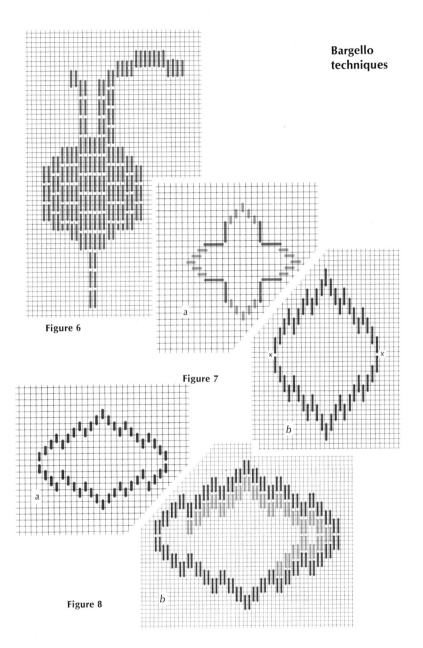

Figure 6

Figure 7

Figure 8

Classification of patterns

Bargello patterns fall into several groups determined by whether the lines are broken or partly broken, whether they are worked as groundings (background repeats), interval fillers, or comprised of uneven-length stitches worked in attached or detached patterns. The four categories can be worked as noted below.

Unbroken line Unbroken-line patterns are characterized by a steady rhythm and are achieved with stitches and steps of even lengths placed in a row (Fig. 9). These patterns are easy to execute, but tend to be monotonous when planned for large surfaces. Unbroken patterns can be dramatic, especially with unusual color harmonies, and are ideally suited for the beginner. For completed example, see Rippling Wave (**1**) in "Notebook of Patterns."

Interval repeat Interval patterns are slightly more difficult to work. They may involve sharing a mesh, use of more than one stitch to a block, or change of line direction with or without change of step. Interval patterns frequently develop secondary motifs between rows of repeats (Fig. 10). See also Strawberry Fields (**29**).

Long and short Commonly known as Hungarian Point, this classification includes patterns worked in rows of single stitches in rhythms of 1 long and 2 short, or combinations of 2 long and 2 short or 1 long and 3 or more short. It is helpful to know that a 1-long-and-2-short rhythm will repeat every third line and may vary in the intermediate lines. Figure 11 illustrates a pattern worked in combinations of long and short stitches with several changes within the repeated rows making up a sequence. Hungarian Point is an ideal method for the design of flower forms, "pagoda roofs" and niches, or draped effects used in

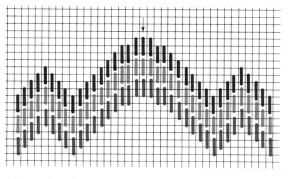

Figure 9

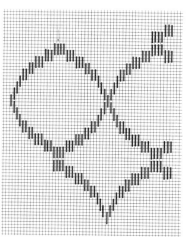

Figure 10

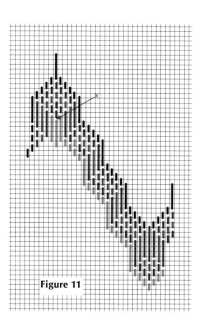

Figure 11

your needle paintings since the contrast of long and short allows shadow play. See also Reflection Variation (**27**).

Groundings   Groundings is a term given to small overall repeat patterns generally used for backgrounds. They offer great opportunity for textural contrasts and perspective. In Figure 12 groundings are used to form a design. They appear as a background in Reflection Variation (**27**).

Honeycombs   These patterns differ from groundings in that their frames are worked in an unbroken line across the canvas. The groundings are then adapted to the voids within the honeycomb frames. Dramatic effects can be achieved with change of color in the unbroken-line frames. Figure 13 shows a honeycomb repeat with grounding filler. See also Cinnebar (**22**).

Detached   Detached patterns are single motifs that can be worked as a device between ribbon bandings, as repeats with groundings, or in combination with other canvas stitches. The flower in Figure 14 can be worked in an alternating reverse or, if balance is desired, another blossom can be added on the opposite side. See Austrian Plissé (**35**) and Pisces (**37**).

Composite   Composite patterns are developed from a central placement of stitches sharing a mesh, generally worked in uneven threads. Figures 15a and b show possible combinations for the center. Note that the division is achieved mostly with shared meshes. Composites can be worked as small interval repeats or as an overall design. See Sunburst (**48**), Star Bright (**52**), Kaleidoscope (**53**).

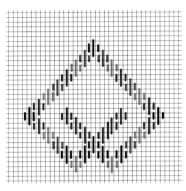

Figure 12

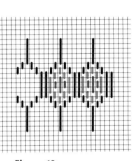

Figure 13

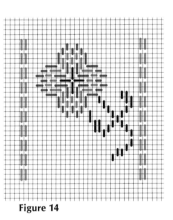

Figure 14

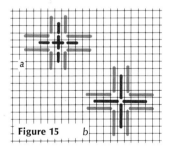

a

Figure 15   b

Needlework shops charge dearly to set up Bargello designs on canvas because of the time and precision required for establishing the pattern tracks. They need not be drawn off on canvas however. The geometric lines can be copied directly with a needle and thread.

This chapter contains guidelines for acquiring needed materials, establishes rules to follow in planning your patterns, gives hints for working them out, and finally, provides advice on blocking and finishing.

Starting on the right track

PREPARING CANVAS

Canvas is not expensive if you buy several yards at a time and cut the material for individual projects as you need it. The best pieces come from the center of the roll. Here the meshes are equally blocked and the threads are strongest. After measuring the amount you need, cut the area to be worked from the center, saving the side pieces for doodle canvas.

Canvas should be bound to prevent fraying before you begin working. Use 1- or 1½-inch wide masking tape. Place canvas on a straight-edged table and with an indelible marker draw a guideline about three quarters of an inch from each edge. Place the tape along the guideline, leaving the second half of the tape to turn under. Reverse the canvas, fold over the tape, and stick it fast to underside of canvas.

To join two pieces of matching canvas, lay the ends of each

canvas together, overlapping about four meshes. Be certain all meshes are lined up evenly and that the selvages run the same way. Baste the two pieces together and work over the two thicknesses with wool.

Canvas threads that have been severed can be mended. If only a few threads are cut, carefully remove the stitches surrounding them with tweezers. Lay the canvas face down on a clean, flat surface. Carefully pull the loose edges together and paint them with clear nail polish. (Ensure that the meshes are not filled with polish by pricking them with a blunt needle while polish is still wet.) Let dry overnight, then work the overlapped area gently with wool. If the hole is large, baste a patch of matching mesh over the hole. Press gently with a steam iron. Work it carefully with matching wool so as not to pull the meshes apart.

Limp canvas may be freshened by applying spray starch to the back.

Work with your canvas resting on a table top and use both hands to regulate tension and shape stitches. If you are working a large, unmounted piece of canvas, roll under the sides up to the area you are working. This will free your hands for front and back work. *Rug canvas should always be worked in this manner.*

Designs worked with varied stitches or on fine-mesh canvas should be mounted on artist's stretchers. *Note that samplers should always be worked on stretchers.* When selecting a stretcher make sure the aperture is 2 inches larger than the finished area of canvas to allow easy access to the embroidery area. Assemble the stretcher and mount the canvas over it using thumbtacks to hold the canvas to the stretcher. Cover the four sides of the mounted canvas with masking tape.

ESTIMATING WOOLS

Once you have selected your design, practice it on a sample doodle canvas. Work a complete sequence using wool scraps, keeping count of the amounts of each color used. To estimate wools needed for your project, measure the completed sequence, determine the number of times it will be repeated to fill your canvas, and multiply the amounts of yarn used in one sequence by the number of repeats. Because dye lots do not always match, invest in extra wool for error (10 percent above the needed amount is enough); save leftover yarns for doodling or darning.

WORKING WITH YARNS AND THREADS

Yarns and threads should be kept in good condition. Use a plastic bag to keep your materials clean. Keep them out of the sun, for heat cooks the oils in the yarn.

Work with short strands of wool, not longer than 16 inches, to avoid fraying. The friction of the canvas on the yarn weakens the fibers and causes the wool to untwist. For uniform strands, measure the length of your skein and cut it open at one end; secure it by tying a strand near the looped end; pull out a single strand as you need it. Leftover pieces of yarn can be wound on cardboard. Tape one end of the yarn to the cardboard, then wind the threads around it.

Wools and threads that have been used and ripped out should not be reworked. They are apt to fuzz up or separate into strands. Remember that your needlework is a permanent work of art and your materials should be as fresh as possible. This is not the time to be frugal: Wool should not be reused after ripping—it should be discarded.

When working with metallic threads, dust your hands lightly with a talcum powder to keep them dry since moisture may oxidize the threads.

Threading the needle   For yarns, the usual method of inserting a single end of thread is not practical since wool is generally more than 1-ply. To thread a needle with wool, loop the wool over the needle and press the loop firmly between thumb and forefinger. Slide loop gently against edge of needle to compress the wool. The flattened loop will go easily through the eye. For metallic threads, select a needle with a large eye, thread one end through the eye, and pull it double. The pull should be gentle to prevent damage to the delicate thread casing.

NOTES ON STITCHERY

To begin a thread leave 1½ inches of wool at the back unknotted. Hold it with your fingers and work the next stitches over it until it is partly covered, taking care not to cut through the wool with your needle. Cut off the loose end. Subsequent threads may be inserted in the back under previously worked areas, but be careful not to stretch the stitches. To end a thread, leave about 2 inches of wool. Work under several stitches on back of canvas and snip off remaining threads closely. Begin and end threads in different areas to avoid ridges.

To stitch, stab the needle vertically through the canvas, avoiding separating previously worked stitches; then pull upward, holding the thread with your left thumb to guide the stitch. The left hand controls tension and will guide threads to evenly placed stitches. It is also useful to correct overlapping or twisted threads.

Correct the position of your stitches as you work. Gently shape them with your needle; rework them if they separate, twist, or bunch. To shape a stitch use the left forefinger, inserting it in the thread loop formed as the needle is stabbed back through the canvas. Guide the loop into a compact, even loop. Check stitches for twisted threads; either correct the twist with your needle or remove the stitch.

If the yarn becomes twisted, drop your needle. Hold up the canvas allowing the needle and thread to fall free; they will unravel themselves. (Watch for twisting especially when working with silk and metallic threads.)

Return to the base of the previous Bargello stitch for the next stitch whenever possible. This gives additional padding to the back and covers the meshes better.

Check the pattern track frequently for errors in stitch length, step length, or missed meshes. In unbroken patterns errors are evident early in the uneven rise and fall of the pattern track. Mistakes in interval patterns are more difficult to spot and these patterns should be examined frequently by running your needle or a hat pin across matching pattern tracks. Correct mistakes at once by removing all stitches to the error point and reworking.

When using several colors or textures, thread each one with a separate needle. After completing a segment, bring the needle with its leftover thread through to the front of the canvas and weave it into open mesh out of the way. This will save time threading needles and make for less thread ends at the back. Watch that ends of contrasting colors do not pull through as you work; tape them at the back for better control.

As the canvas may not always be covered, compensation stitches can be worked over your threads. This is particularly true when different types of stitches are worked next to each other. Always work the compensation stitches after the entire pattern track is finished to be certain that the filler stitches do not break the pattern.

Go over your finished work carefully to see that all canvas threads are covered. A single strand of matching thread can be worked over a stitch to cover any exposed area.

TRANSFERRING PATTERNS TO CANVAS

With Bargello patterns, it is not necessary to reproduce your design directly on the canvas. Instead, draw your design on graph paper of the same scale as your canvas. If corresponding graph paper is not available, the squares of the paper should be half the number of canvas meshes. For instance, if you work on No. 16 canvas, graph paper should be 8 to the inch. After drawing your design, count the stitches and steps on the graph paper and reproduce them with stitches on the canvas.

Tracing needlepoint designs on canvas   To trace a pattern directly on the canvas, place the design face up under the canvas and tape the edges of the pattern and canvas together. Then with the canvas side facing you, tape the design to a sunny window. Using an indelible pen in lighter colors than the yarns to be used, trace the pattern outlines.

Another method is to use a glass-topped table with a lamp under it. Place the design on the table surface with the canvas on top. The lamplight will throw the design into sharp profile, making it easy to trace.

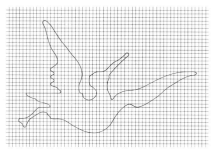

Enlarging or reducing patterns   If the design is not the size you need, it can be reduced or enlarged. You may do this yourself with the aid of a pantograph or, if you prefer, the design can be reduced or enlarged by a professional photostater.

Another way of changing the size of a given pattern is to use the squaring method. Using transparent graph paper, trace the design inside a square drawn on the paper, using one-half or one-quarter squares to the inch for small patterns. On a second sheet of graph paper, grade the squares according to the size you wish the finished design to be. Transfer each portion of the design within a square on the smaller-grid graph paper to the corresponding square of the larger-grid graph paper (Fig. 1).

Reversing a pattern   To reverse a design, make a tracing of it. Over your canvas place a piece of nonsmudge dressmaker's carbon. On top of the carbon, place your tracing, making sure the wrong side of the tracing is facing you. Retrace the outline, and remove tracing and dressmaker's carbon. The reverse design now appears on your canvas.

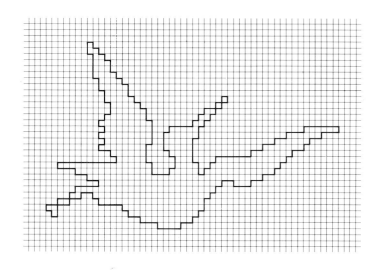

Figure 1

20

Proper pattern placement is essential in Bargello. Motifs are usually centered and repeats are uniform top to bottom, side to side. To place your design accurately, use a ruler to line off a square 2 inches inside masking tape border. Count threads along one row at top and mark center with an indelible pen or thread. Using a different color, mark the centers of both sides and bottom. Count the number of threads or meshes diagonally and vertically, locate the center of the canvas, and mark as above.

Graph paper is recommended for working out the placement of complicated designs but the following general hints apply to the centering of various design classifications. Arrows on graphs show starting center stitch.

Unbroken line To set up the track of an unbroken-line pattern, determine the center of the pattern. Work the center stitch in the mesh below the center mark at the top of the canvas. Work from this stitch to the right, repeating the pattern track from the middle stitch and ending at the right margin of the canvas. Work left side of canvas margin (Fig. 2). Check for errors. Once you have established this lead track or row for an unbroken-line pattern, you merely repeat it in subsequent rows changing colors as indicated. Some unbroken-line patterns complete their track in more than one row. Check carefully and set the pattern track accordingly.

Interval repeat These tracks are also set up from the center of the canvas. Count the meshes of the interval repeat horizontally and vertically and center the outline in the middle of the canvas (Fig. 3). To prevent errors in pattern placement, establish and work all other outline tracks for the interval pattern before you fill them in. After the outlines are worked on the canvas complete their filler segments, checking for accuracy as you work. Segments of the pattern may repeat only partially at margins; watch that these segments are uniform.

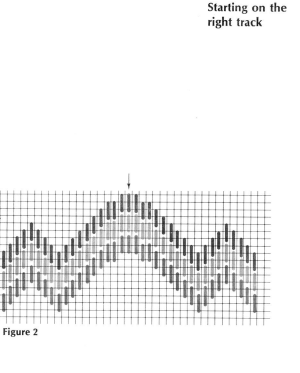

Figure 2

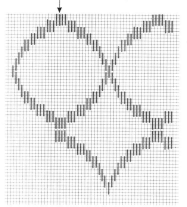

Figure 3

Long and short A complete pattern sequence involving long and short steps should be worked out on graph paper, noting the track of each row. These rows often change in a pattern cycle, taking several rows to complete the pattern, varying in step count and number of stitches (Fig. 4). The peaks of the pattern track adjust to accommodate the changing rhythms of long and short stitches, but within a preset number of rows the first pattern track starts a repeat (see point X). Use a knitting counter to help you pick up the proper row. After you have centered the first row, you can work from left to right provided you have mastered the changes of the pattern track, but it is essential to complete the track before starting the repeat.

Groundings When worked as overall patterns, groundings are started from center top like unbroken-line patterns and are also worked right and left toward margins. The second row may be started under any stitch of the first row, provided the meshing of the pattern segments does not alter the design (Fig. 5). The track can be worked horizontally or vertically once you are familiar with the meshing of the pattern track. Where several colors are used in a grounding, you can complete a thread of one color by working different segments. A full row should be completed before working in segments; this offers a constant check and ensures that your pattern is in proper repeat.

Honeycombs These designs have frames that are worked as unbroken-line patterns. One honeycomb is centered in the first row of the pattern track; the row is then worked to right margin. Return to the center honeycomb and work to left margin (Fig. 6). Count the numbers of rows between the first row of the frame and the last; repeat this interval of voids between first and bottom rows of the honeycomb frame. Center the pattern track under the first row and work to right and left margins; this will provide frames for the honeycombs. After all the frames are completed, work their grounding fillers from the center of the frame out to its edges.

22

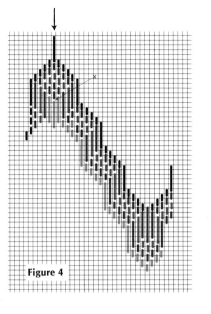

Figure 4

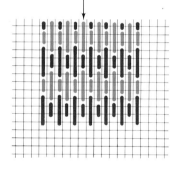

Figure 5

Figure 6

Detached Since detached patterns are often worked in ribbons of supplementary design devices, framed in latticework,
planned as accents for backgrounds or groundings, it is wise to
draw the completed composition on graph paper using a grid
to match the meshes of your canvas. This will give you the exact
size for the repeat and you can place the pattern track on the
canvas using the detached motif in as many repeats as are al-
lowed by the size of your piece. The placement of the pattern
track will depend on the number of repeats you intend to use.
Here ribbons are worked first, followed by detached repeats,
then background (Fig. 7).

Composites These designs are worked from the center of the
canvas, developing their shapes as the pattern track directs.
They may be worked as a central motif, bordered by another
stitch, or scaled to fill the entire canvas by repeating the stitch
sequence until the margins are reached (Fig. 8).

Basically the stitches are stepped, sharing a mesh to extend
the pattern track. The pattern will develop in fins with corridors
between them. After the fins are worked to the border the corridors are worked in long and short stitches, stepped to fit the
area.

BLOCKING AND FINISHING

When your design is completed, work a few extra rows around
the canvas to allow for the seams to turn under. Run extra
strands of matching yarns and threads through the back of the
canvas to be used for future repairs. (They will be subjected to
the same blocking and cleaning, and consequently to the same
color fading as the finished piece.)

Certain Bargello patterns shrink more than others and you
should allow for this by working enough canvas to compensate.
Upright stitches shrink vertically. Work a repeat on your
doodle canvas and block it to ascertain its shrinkage ratio. This

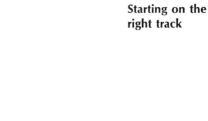

Figure 7

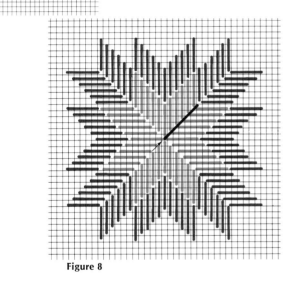

Figure 8

23

is especially important when making rugs because the pieces must be joined at matching meshes.

Do not trim away excess canvas; it will unravel. Your upholsterer will cut it when he mounts the piece. After it has been mounted, a missed stitch can be reworked with a curved upholsterer's needle and matching threads.

If you can't find a suitable fabric or leather backing for finishing your pillow, try simulating a piece of fabric using the colors from your needlework piece and a quick Bargello pattern.

Professional upholsterers or framers will block, mount, or finish your piece for you. Their prices vary and can be quite costly but their professional touch is often worth the price, especially if you have invested time and talent in the unblocked piece and feel insecure about finishing it yourself. You should, however, know how to explain to the finisher what you wish done with your piece. He will want to know the type of lining, trimming, seams, and filling you desire.

Blocking   Needlework may get out of shape while you are working it, but careful blocking will correct this problem. Blocking is the process of reshaping through wetting and stretching that is necessary before the piece is mounted. If the piece has become badly distorted it may take more than one blocking to straighten it out.

The materials needed for blocking are a clean, smooth plywood board larger than your project, pushpins to hold the canvas, and a ruler and T square to true up the edges. (It is useful before you work your piece to make an outline of it on the blocking board with waterproof pen.) Using a basin of clean, cold water and a sponge, pat work gently, wetting just enough to moisten it but not enough to soak it. The water will release the sizing in the canvas and your hands may get sticky. Lay the blocking board on a flat surface so that the sizing will not run down through the canvas and streak the design. After the canvas is evenly moistened, use rustproof pushpins to tack the

canvas to the board. Start tacking at the middle of each side and work toward the corners. If you work all four sides together the pull will be more even. Try to bring the canvas to the squared outline of the marks on the board. The pushpins should be placed about 1 inch apart and about 1 inch from the edge of the pattern area. When all sides are pulled tightly and securely tacked with the pushpins set the blocking board in a horizontal position to dry. It will take from several days to a week, depending upon the size of the canvas and the room's humidity. It is important that needlework dry away from artificial heat and direct sunlight to prevent shrinkage of yarn, preferably in a cool dry place with good air circulation. When completely dry remove the pushpins. Blocking will flatten the stitches slightly; if you wish to fluff them up, hold a steam iron a few inches above the canvas and gently steam the surface, taking care the iron does not touch it.

Careful planning should go into the mounting of your needlework. No picture frame should be ordered until the canvas is completely dry and has been remeasured.

Finishing   The following hints will assist you in planning your finishing whether you do it yourself or enlist the aid of a professional.

Down-filled pillows are preferred because they adapt easily to the soft contours of needlework and are long lasting. Foam rubber pillows tend to look stiff and the material disintegrates in time.

Commercial fringes and trimmings, although available, seldom come in the right color combinations suitable for your needlework. A fringe can be made by combining different widths of edgings and a ball fringe to an assemblage that matches your pillow in color and texture. Measure around the four edges and add an extra 4 inches for corner turns.

PRINCIPLES OF DESIGN
AND THEIR APPLICATION

Language of design

Design is a language by which we communicate creative ideas to our fellow man. It is a treasure house of stored information, preserving records of the cultures of previous generations. Many patterns used today in Bargello stitchery have their origins in fifteenth-century motifs.

Those wishing to do original or creative work will find stimuli to new ideas in the variety of ways in which the articulate tools of design can be combined. These elements of design include color, rhythm, repetition, transition, texture, contrast, line direction, dominance and accent, balance, and scale and proportion. The purpose of this chapter is to teach you to recognize each of them, to further your understanding of how they affect each other, and to encourage you to use them in creating new designs.

The elements of design

COLOR

Color is the most compelling element of design and in Bargello the most active one. To make the most of color in creating designs you should have a working knowledge of its vocabulary and qualities. Color is the nerve response to light as it enters the eye, and these responses perform the functions described below.

Functions of color

Color defines the outline or limits of objects such as the petals of a rose, the points of a snowflake, or the beginnings of a border. It also dictates the physical condition of certain objects, for example, ripe fruit versus unripe fruit.

Color recalls psychological associations, that is, our experiences, traditions, and symbolic images. For example, green indicates gardens, grass, unripened fruit, youth, leaves of trees and plants, or perhaps St. Patrick's Day. The familiar red and green traffic lights at intersections tell us when to stop and when to go. Red may indicate danger, anger, the excitement of a bullfight, the center of a target or, when combined with green, may remind us of Christmas. Yellow and orange bring to mind sunflowers, daffodils, sunlight, tropical fruit, or the rich, throbbing colors of a Gauguin painting. Blue brings visions of sky, water, certain flowers, or the delicate shadings of a Monet painting. Violet is used by nature for shadows and to vein or tint flowers and trees. Grapes, plums, eggplants, and beets all contain some chroma of violet in their pigments. Violet is also the color of royalty and Easter. Be conscious of such color associations as you seek the right color harmonies.

Color stimulates us to enrich our surroundings by creating a personal atmosphere or mood, reflecting the emotionally colorful climate in which we wish to live. The decorative function of color-consciousness is of great value in coordinating needlework with interiors.

Qualities of color

The vocabulary of color uses certain terms to describe its qualities. Familiarize yourself with them to become fluent in color communication.

Value is the lightness or darkness of a color.

Tints are lighter hues of a color. They are formed by adding white to a color.

Shades of a color are produced by adding black to the color.

Tones of a color are produced by adding gray to the color.

Color scale is composed of the tints, shades, and tones of a color. (The word *scale* is easy to remember because *scala* is the Latin word for ladder, and the gradation of the scale represents a ladder of color.)

Hue means the family to which a color belongs.

Chroma of a color is its fullest intensity.

Visual aids to the study of color

Color wheel The spectrum reflected by means of a glass prism held in direct sunlight will contain red, orange, yellow, green, blue, and violet hues. In the prism state the colors of the spectrum will fuse. Separate them into a circle or wheel as shown in Figure 1 and you have a working guide for forming color harmonies.

Working from the color wheel you will be able to create a color chart containing the spectrum colors with their tints and shades. Add white to the spectrum colors in ever-increasing amounts and you will achieve tints. Conversely, working with the same spectrum hues, by adding black, shades will be created. All tints and shades will still possess the same qualities and perform the same functions as the color of the original hue. Add gray to the spectrum color and tones will result.

Note that on the color wheel the three primary colors—red, blue, and yellow—are equal distances apart. Secondary colors are mixed from these primary colors. They are:

Red and yellow equals orange
Blue and yellow equals green
Red and blue equals violet.

Mix a primary and secondary color and the result is a tertiary color. The tertiaries are:

Red plus orange equals red orange

Figure 1

Red plus violet equals red violet
Yellow plus green equals yellow green
Yellow plus orange equals yellow orange
Blue plus violet equals blue violet
Blue plus green equals blue green.

Color harmonies

Devised by M. E. Chevreul in 1870, color harmonies are produced by accepted associations which are classified as related or contrasting harmonies.

Color harmonies   Related harmonies are divided into monochromatic and analogous harmonies.

Monochromatic harmonies are composed of restrained and recessive colors consisting of the use of one color with its tints and shades. For example, see Pink Parfait (**3**).*

Analogous harmonies are composed of colors adjoining each other on the color wheel and are related through one primary color, e.g., red, red orange, and orange. See Sunburst (**48**). The analogous harmony is one of nature. When the harmony is formed by using warm colors, such as reds, yellows, and oranges, it is cheerful and dominant; when cool blues, greens, and violets are used, it becomes recessive as in Rose Window (**15**).

Contrasting color harmonies   This type of color harmony can be obtained by the use of direct complements, split complements, triadic harmonies, or paired complements.

Direct complements are colors opposite each other on the color wheel, e.g., blue and orange, red and green, yellow and

* Throughout this chapter names are cited from the "Notebook of Patterns" to show examples of color relationships. These patterns appear chronologically in order of difficulty and the number in parentheses refers to sequence.

violet. Complementary colors are best used in unequal quantities, with one color dominating the other. Nature uses these harmonies with their monochromatic tints and shades as in the pink rose with green leaves. Complementary harmonies used in full intensity become strident and bold, modern in feeling as in Lollypop Trees Variation (**10**). When used with tints and shades they become delicate and dainty as in the pink and green of Star Bright (**52**).

Split complements are obtained by using one color with the two colors immediately adjacent to its direct complement. For example, red is used with blue green and yellow green in Kaleidoscope (**53**).

Triadic harmonies are formed by the use of any three colors forming an equilateral triangle on the color wheel such as blue, pink, and yellow in Brocade (**40**).

Paired complements involve the use of pairs of direct complements. They are most effective when used with one pair of complements dominant, the other recessive. See Grapevine Espalier (**43**) for yellow, purple, red, green.

Notes on color

☐ Use neutrals, black, white, and gray to achieve separation in color bands. Use them for outline, accent, or dominance.

☐ Knowledge of the scale of a color will help in shading leaves, flowers, shadow forms, and in creating multidimensional effects.

☐ The shadows of a form should reflect the tones of the colors used in the form. Check your color scale for the proper shades to use.

☐ When in doubt about what color to use for shadow effect use the darkest intensity of the color to be shadowed. For example, brown is the darkest shade of orange so an orange form should be shadowed by one of the shades of brown. Creating shadows for forms in needlework is an excellent way of making your work original. Study the shadows in nature as they fall and learn their directions.

When light strikes a chair, the shadows will never completely surround the chair; they will lie in related positions to the shadows
of surrounding forms according to the way the light strikes them.

☐ Wallpapers, fabrics, wrapping papers, and floor tiles have fine examples of color harmonies created by designers who are knowl-
edgeable about color combinations. Study their designs and create
your own ideas from their harmonies.

RHYTHM

Rhythm is the path the eye follows as it works its way through
a design. Rhythm creates activity, it brings the design to life,
and its motion usually requires the assistance of other elements,
namely, repetition and transition.

Functions of rhythm

Rhythm should provide measured, proportional intervals of
color within a pattern. By changing these measured, proportional intervals of color, we create *color chords*. In turn, these
color chords will have a second interval established by the areas
existing between their bands. The planning of such areas between the bands of color chords is known as *rhythm interval
designing*. Rhythm also functions with changes in line direction
to create a form with motion. It can also be used to emphasize
the effect of scale through increasing or decreasing the measured proportional intervals.

Techniques for rhythm changes

By altering the number of stitches in a block or sequence or by
alterations in the "step" of the chord rhythms, the rhythm of a
pattern may be changed. See Sea Nymph (**7**).

The direction of an established rhythm may be changed. In Figure 2 a simple rhythm forms a pattern. See Rippling Wave (**1**). Also in Figure 2 the same rhythm has its direction reversed in the repeat to form an interval pattern. See Rondel (**2**).

As mentioned above, rhythm can influence design by continuing the path the eye follows, or by arresting it with a break. Figure 3a and b shows rhythm arrested and unarrested. Rhythm is arrested with the aid of accent or dominance. In Figure 3b it is the change in the blocks of stitches at the peaks and valleys known as accent that arrests the rhythm. Figure 3c shows the arrest of rhythm by dominance.

By utilizing transition, we can also effect a rhythm change. When the transition from light to dark, from dull to bright, or from small to large is gradual, we say that rhythm is working with transition to bring a change in pattern. These transitional changes can be gradual as in Figure 4a which shows "thicks and thins" or with the aid of abrupt contrast as is shown in Figure 4b.

It is also possible to change the rhythm by resting at a point and changing direction. Such changes in line direction (often achieved in Bargello by sharing a mesh) offer interesting new patterns as is shown in Figure 5. Such changes in rhythm should be carefully planned so that fragmentation of certain areas or interference with the overall unity of the design is avoided. Figure 6 shows a pattern created by changing the line direction of rhythm to form corridors. The black lines offer rhythm paths for the eye to peruse.

Rhythm, as it directs the eye throughout the design, controls the unity of many of the other elements it works with. In Figure 7a broken segments are scattered at random in a field without any rhythm. Figure 7b shows rhythm employed as a unifying agent programming the independent segments into a cross. The unorganized elements in Figure 7a are the same size, color, and form as those of their companion controlled by rhythm. Many interesting composite designs can be formed by unifying segments of different sizes and shapes.

32

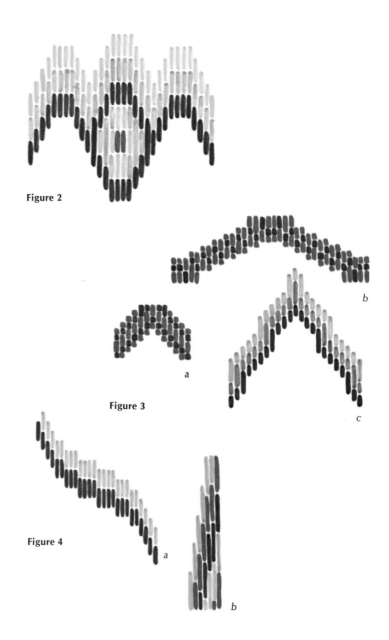

Figure 2

Figure 3

a

b

c

Figure 4

a

b

Notes on rhythm

☐ Working with folded paper cutouts will help you to learn how to unify segments of a design.
☐ The neutrals, black, white, and gray can be used in interval areas between color chords to break the rhythm and to vary the pattern. See Sea Nymph (7).
☐ Rhythm should not be restless but should have pulse, pace, and purpose. It should unify and not fragment the overall pattern.

Figure 5

REPETITION

Repetition is the number of times an element is repeated within a design, and is the essence of rhythm. It is also the design device used most often for unification. By repeating the color, texture, or line direction the composition takes on a related whole. In nature we are familiar with repetition in the ebb and flow of tides, of night and day, waning and waxing of the moon —all are eternally repeating the cycle of the balance of nature.

Figure 6

Functions of repetition

The varied repetition seen in nature's snowflakes is produced by repeating one or more aspects with a change in direction, size, or form. In needlework we vary repetition also with color and textural changes, aided by transition.

Techniques of repetition

To vary repetition we can invert the design as is done in Rondel (2) and Aubusson Symphony (41), reverse it as is shown in the marigolds in Pennsylvania Dutch (38), or alternate the design as is done in the bands of French Ribbon (24).

Exact repetition may have a soothing effect but in the ab-

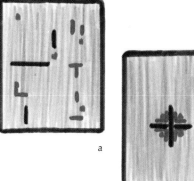

a

Figure 7

b

sence of any variation it becomes monotonous. In needlework, exact repetition benefits by interchange of sequence, i.e., from dark to light, light to dark as in Rippling Wave (**1**).

Notes on repetition

☐ Repetition of forms benefits by changes in size and shape. For example, see the changes in peaks in Alpine Slopes (**12**).
☐ Color may be repeated with changes in texture and stitch size as is done in Coral Reef (**6**).
☐ The repetition of the neutrals white, black, and gray may be introduced into color chords to relieve monotony. An effective use of neutrals is seen in Pomegranate Variation (**13**).

TRANSITION

Transition is the element that regulates the degree of change in color, form, or texture. It may work independently of rhythm to create depth and perspective.

Functions of transition

One function of transition is to aid rhythm in creating motion by instituting gradual changes in color, form, or texture of a design. To achieve a change in color, color chords can be varied by using closely related tints, tones, and shades.

Transition also works with contrast to create forms. If color continues row after row in closely related transitions a rainbow effect is achieved. If this transition is abrupt, the resulting contrast can be employed as shown in Figure 8. Note that the enclosed void achieved by the abrupt transition becomes a niche with depth; this device can be used effectively as a background for a new design device. See Deep Boxes Variation (**9**).

The steps of the design are also influenced by transition. If

Figure 8

the step is gradual the rhythm of the design will be regular and restful. If the transition is abrupt in the step (stepping up or down in long intervals), dominance will join transition and the eye will come to rest at the point of the longest interval. Too abrupt a transition in a step gives the effect of sharp points or fangs, resulting in a dramatic rather than restful pattern.

Transition can also be achieved by textural change in Bargello, and it aids in the relating of silk and metallic threads to wool through color gradation.

Notes on transition

☐ The number of threads covered in one stitch should be planned with good transition in mind. If the change in length of stitches is erratic, the flow of rhythm will be confused. In Figures 9a and 9b examples of good and poor transition are shown.

☐ In Figure 9a the change in number of stitches to a block is gradual, and the changes are separated by an accent interval of repeated stitches that act as stepping-stones to lead the eye through the design.

☐ In Figure 9b the changes in stitch number in a block is abrupt, the contrast between the blocks of stitches too great, and the rhythm is too erratic.

☐ Transition of textures should be carefully planned to avoid too busy an effect. Often only a highlight of silk or metallic thread is needed to offer a textural change.

☐ The goal of all good design is unity, and to explore this unity a path is needed. Transition provides such a path and therefore it should not be interrupted by unrelated forms, colors, or textures unless they are germaine to the overall unity.

TEXTURE

The tissue structure of the material used is referred to as its texture. This may be influenced by processing methods and be smooth, glossy, rough, or dull. Texture is visual as well as tactile,

a

b

Figure 9

because glossy surfaces reflect more light than dull or matte surfaces. The same color may appear differently when smooth, rough, or metallic in texture. Because of these visual aspects, texture has an important function in relieving the monotony of a design. The introduction of new materials has caused texture to become a versatile element in modern design, perhaps the element with the most potential for exploration in the designing of needlework.

Functions of texture

To prevent monotony in rhythm, a well-planned variety of thread textures may be used. One difficulty in introducing several textures is that when introduced as an agent of accent or dominance a texture can cause the rhythm to break off, thus diminishing the effectiveness of the overall pattern.

When utilized for balance to give greater visual weight to an asymmetrical design, texture lends stability to the composition. Texture also provides a realistic note by simulating the actual composition of the original subject. For example, rough threads can be used for tree bark and delicate, smooth threads for a soft rosebud.

By working entirely in one texture, unity can be achieved by allowing the design to develop through the transition of stitch lengths, color, or line direction.

Exquisite designs simulating cameos (forms used as background in low relief) or intaglio motifs (forms incised or countersunk) can be effected by using one texture and varying the stitch length and direction. See Victoria (**56**); Quilting Bee (**44**).

Notes on texture

☐ The textures of a particular object should be designed with the object's ultimate use in mind. For example, silk or metallic threads because of their fragility should not be used for a footstool.
☐ Needles with appropriately sized eyes should be used to avoid fraying nubby or tubular thread textures.
☐ Textural materials too thick for needle stitchery, such as cording, braid, or string, can be couched into the design.
☐ Textural material should be related to the rest of the composition through color or transition.

CONTRAST

Contrast is the dynamic element of a pattern and is used to enliven a design. It is axiomatic in good design to employ contrasts. There are degrees of contrast: It may be opposite, nearly opposite, unlike, similar with variety, or in conflict. The greater the contrast the more dynamic the effect. Contrast is achieved by emphasizing the difference between a segment of a design and the elements near it. Without using some contrast, repetition becomes monotonous. However, contrast should be used with restraint since the use of too many contrasting elements disturbs unity, the goal of all good design. Contrast is like the salt in our diet and its use is governed by our personal taste.

Functions of contrast

Contrast of line direction creates forms and lends visual activity to a design. In a design utilizing repetition of line, contrast may be achieved by varying the size of a line and its direction (Fig. 10).

Contrast of both texture and color may be used. For example, see Brocade (**40**), where such a contrast combination is used to create shadow play.

Interest is produced by variety. Within a given composition there will be major and minor intervals. Such intervals should be kept unequal in impact, since equal intervals create monotony. When contrast is properly used, it balances the major and minor intervals within a composition as in Figure 11.

See Persian Mosque (**39**) for example of line variation, shadow play, and interval contrasts.

Note on contrast

☐ Vary the unequal contrasts between elements in a composition. For example, a composition equally divided into two blocks of red and green offers little for the eye. The same composition worked against a neutral background of white, black, or gray, in blocks of uneven sizes and different colors (pink and dark green), and in different textures (silk with a metallic thread border or wool with a silk border) invites us to evaluate the contrasts.

LINE DIRECTION

A line may be broken or it may be two- or three-dimensional as in a bent twig. The contour of a line's undulating surface creates patterns as it intersects planes. A line may be weak, strong, firm, thin, soft, or blurred.

Functions of line direction

Lines denote directional changes, i.e., horizontal, vertical, or oblique. Horizontal lines denote harmony as they pull with gravity. Vertical lines suggest poise, strength, and balance. Oblique lines are transitional, dynamic, and often insecure by themselves. They usually require support of an opposite diagonal or right-angled line for good design.

Lines express moods as in the gay swirling lines of a dancing skirt. A jagged line with abrupt and frequent change of direction gives a nervous and erratic effect. Lines can be used to create a form as in a leaf or flower. (See Fig. 12.)

Lines have qualities of rhythm as in the break of a wave.

Figure 10

Figure 11

Figure 12

Notes on line direction

☐ Horizontal and vertical lines are combined in Bargello by sharing a mesh. All directional changes in lines are achieved in this manner.
☐ Textural changes between outline stitches and filler stitches create depth and dimension in a line.
☐ Lines with undulating surfaces make effective border treatments.

DOMINANCE AND ACCENT

Dominance is represented by one feature to which all else is subordinated. It is most skillfully used when it unifies other elements. In needlework it is represented by unusual textures, stitches, colors, or forms. It brings the eye to a full stop as it wends its way through the path of the design.

Accent differs from dominance in being less forceful. It creates stepping-stones to help your eye work its way along the design path; it may slow down but does not completely stop the line direction. Both accent and dominance are important tools in creating new design patterns. In Figures 13 and 14 examples of designs created with accent and dominance are shown. (Note that the accent stitches in Fig. 13 act as stepping-stones of color as they guide the eye through the field of green, whereas in Fig. 14 dominance arrests the eye by offering a pause in the pursuit of pattern.)

Functions of dominance and accent

Dominance and accent call attention to areas of importance in the design. When used to break up vast background areas, accent repeats are effective in relieving monotony, such as in Tiffany Favrile (**49**) background of the contrasting yellow and orange. Dominance and accent aid balance by increasing visual

Figure 13

Figure 14

weight in an area of the pattern and they can also be used to divide areas of design to aid in proportion.

Notes on dominance and accent

☐ Good design consists of more than just filling an area. By the judicious use of dominance and accent, the background area can be made more interesting. Care must be taken, however, to assure that the background variations remain of secondary importance to the main design elements.

☐ When dominance is overused, the forms created by the dominant form compete with the other elements in the pattern. When doubtful about the effect of using dominance in a particular design, avoid its use altogether and try accenting the area instead. Remember that contrast and dominance work with scale and proportion to give balance to areas.

☐ A study of Figures 15a and *b* which show respectively good and poor dominance will help the novice to avoid disappointments.

☐ Some gifted people instinctively use design elements to their greatest advantage, while others learn by observing good and poor examples of the elements at work.

☐ A frequent error of beginners is to overuse dominance as a design concept. Many novices erroneously assume that if dominance is used well once, it is even better repeated in a second band. However, by repeating such bands they cease to be dominant but become a pattern repeat against the background and, in fact, they lack dominance in their design relationship.

☐ In stitchery the backgrounds become voids. If these voids are too vast and unbroken, the center field of the design is difficult to scale to the background. Break up the background void with a different stitch, a change of texture, or an accent repeat.

☐ Using a border pattern as an accent motif is another way to relate the center field to the background in proportion and scale.

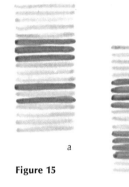

a

Figure 15

b

BALANCE

Balance is the division of elements about a central axis so there will be equal visual weight on either side of the axis. Balance can be symmetrical as shown in Figure 16a where equal physical weight is placed on both sides of the axis. Or it can be asymmetrical as is shown in Figure 16b.

The line direction of the design, whether stable or agitated, defines the plane distribution and in so doing influences the type of balance used. For example, if the line's kinetic direction and agitated movement divide the planes unequally about the central axis, asymmetrical balance ensues and compensation for the visual weight of these planes must be developed to achieve a feeling of repose and equilibrium. An example of such an effect can be seen in waves as they are pictured in Japanese prints.

A calligraphic line is often informal and may be emotional. But whether it crawls or scampers gaily across the surface it divides the planes, and in so doing demands a balance of the segmented parts, this balance depending on the relationship of the newly formed segments.

The strong vertical line is more demanding; though it soars it suggests stability. Since it is more difficult to use as an asymmetrical balance device, a beginner would benefit by using this uncompromising line with a symmetrical distribution of solids and voids.

Figure 16

Functions of balance

The main function of balance is to lend stability to a composition. Such stability is easily achieved when the elements are equally duplicated on both sides of a central axis. Though more difficult to achieve, asymmetrical balance is just as effective in stabilizing a design.

Asymmetrical balance allows you to develop the areas on either side of the central axis with elements of equal visual, but not necessarily of equal physical, weight. For instance, the visual weight of a smaller form when worked in a dominant color balances with a larger form worked in a less dominant color. Remember that the line direction of the design, whether stable or agitated, influences the type of balance used.

Notes on balance

☐ Balance is best achieved by careful planning. Either make a graph of the design or use folded paper cutouts to establish the balance on both sides of the central axis.

☐ Since the visual weight of colors varies, the cutouts or graph should be colored to ensure proper balance.

☐ Watch the background voids since they may be developed into secondary forms or shadows influencing the visual weights of the overall pattern.

SCALE AND PROPORTION

Scale and proportion are the elements that regulate form: When these elements balance, the resultant form is pleasing, but when they are unbalanced, the opposite effect is achieved.

Scale is the size-relationship of the component parts of a composition. By using measured relationships between the elements, good scale is obtained.

Proportion is the size-relationship of the completed design as a whole. Proportion in the design should be related to the ultimate use of the finished piece. For example, the forms in the design of the chair cover should be in proportion to the furniture it covers, the forms in the belt design should be in proportion to the waist it encircles, or in the case of a needle painting, the design should be in proportion to the wall on which it hangs.

Functions of scale and proportion

New patterns can be created in Bargello by changing the scale within the design. Figure 17a shows a design which is altered

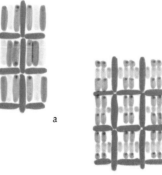

a

b

Figure 17

in 17*b* by changing the scale relationship of stitches sharing a mesh. See also Kaleidoscope (**53**).

The use of scale and proportion for needle painting is shown in Persian Mosques (**39**). By varying scale or proportions many classical patterns can be the basis for modern designs.

New ideas for designs can be evolved from the division of solids and voids with special attention given to the relationship of scale and proportion. These ideas can be worked on graph paper or on canvas, the surface dealt with being regulated by the outline of the borders (Fig. 18).

Further interest can be developed within the surface divisions with change in stitch direction, textural and color changes, or as shown in Figure 19, by balancing a dominant form with lawns of stitches, corridors of color, and stepping-stones of contrast. This is an excellent way to make an embroidery record of your garden.

By varying the proportions of composites, new patterns can be created. See Star Bright (**52**) and Kaleidoscope (**53**).

Figure 18

Notes on scale and proportion

☐ Noting the proportions that nature establishes will lend stability to your designs. For example, the proportion of the stem to the flower, the grapes in a bunch, or the width of color bars in a rainbow.
☐ Using block-building techniques will create equal proportions.

Changing and adapting patterns

Changing and adapting patterns is simple once you have some knowledge of the basic elements in the language of design. Drawing skill is not necessary to create new patterns. As you familiarize yourself with the elements of design you will de-

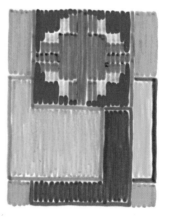

Figure 19

velop a "seeing eye." This eye will enable you to discover patterns in paintings, pictures in books, and commercial art and to pick from them the basic ideas you wish to work with. Often this is a matter of disregarding their covering motifs and using their structural material combined with your own creative ideas. Patterns can be adapted or changed as noted below.

The use of embroidery patterns Many embroidery patterns can be adapted to Bargello as shown in Figures 20a and b where butterfly and bud forms traced on graph paper are then adapted to blocks of stitches. Such forms make excellent over-all repeat patterns placed at intervals on a neutral field. They work well between stripes of ribbon needlework as shown in Austrian Plissé (**35**). As motifs in needle painting they offer accent. By adapting the motif for a left or a right profile, an over-all repeat pattern can have added interest.

The use of natural forms Leaves, flowers, and other natural forms can be traced on graph paper and adapted to Bargello by using the same method of block stitches that was used for adapting embroidery patterns (Fig. 21). Pictures and cartoons of natural forms can be traced on graph paper and adapted to blocks of stitches. Attention should be given to shadowing of the forms to make them realistic.

The use of counter-change Design changes can be wrought through counter-change, i.e., the reversing of field and figure coloring. Figure 22 shows an example of the effective use of counter-change.

The use of folded paper cutouts Cutout assemblages made from folded paper offer greater variety because their segments can be altered or shifted easily.

The use of natural, functional, and cultural harmonies Stability

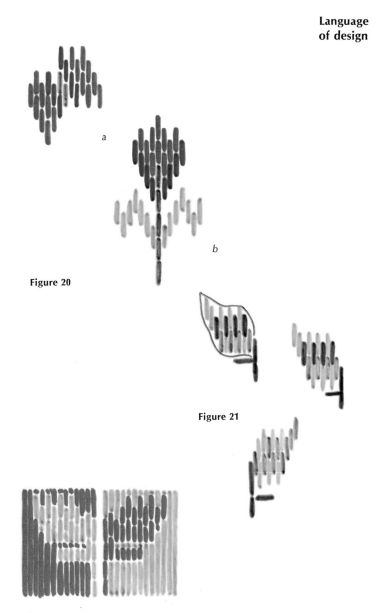

a

b

Figure 20

Figure 21

Figure 22

can be achieved in your first design attempts by making use of natural harmonies. For example, use a combination of fish and wave forms or flower and leaf forms. Observe functional harmonies in nature and make use of your observations when placing objects together. For example, use fruits and flowers in a basket, flowers in a vase. Cultural objects can also be adapted to a design such as a dove with an olive branch, the vertical designs of a totem pole, or the stylized figures of Egyptian hieroglyphics or Chinese calligraphy.

ADAPTING DESIGNS BY SQUARING

Ornate patterns often contain small design motifs that prove to be jewels lost in the overall detail. Enlarge them by squaring (see p. 20), and use them as a central motif or in a repeat.

ADAPTING DESIGNS BY ABSTRACTION

Bargello is particularly suitable for abstraction because it uses blocks of stitches to achieve a pattern. In Figures 23a and b a wine bottle, glass, and grapes have been adapted through abstraction to Bargello.

ADAPTING DESIGNS WITH THE USE OF BUILDING BLOCKS

Pagodas, buildings, scenes, human figures, animals, or any motif having proportionate ratios can easily be reproduced in Bargello by using stitches in matching or complementing blocks. Figure 24 shows an Oriental scene complete with pagoda, man, trees, and a duck in water that was created with building blocks. This design can be worked in monochromatic harmonies or in neutral colors. It is a useful design where a piece is to be worked in tints and shades of one color.

Figure 23

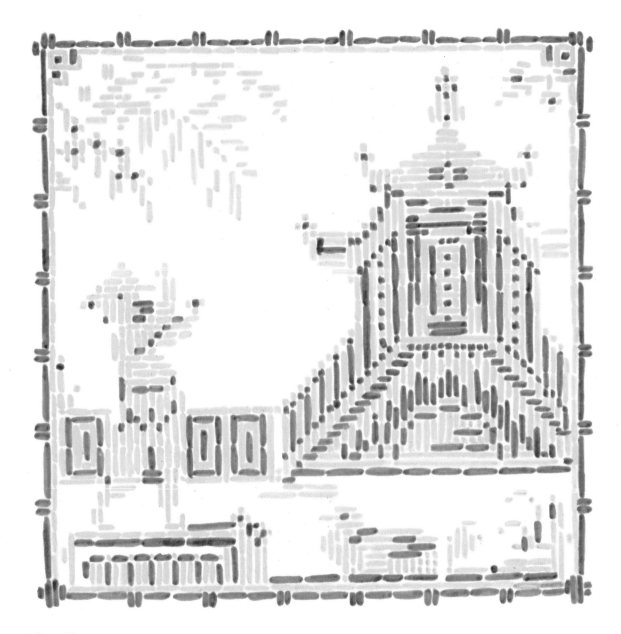

Figure 24

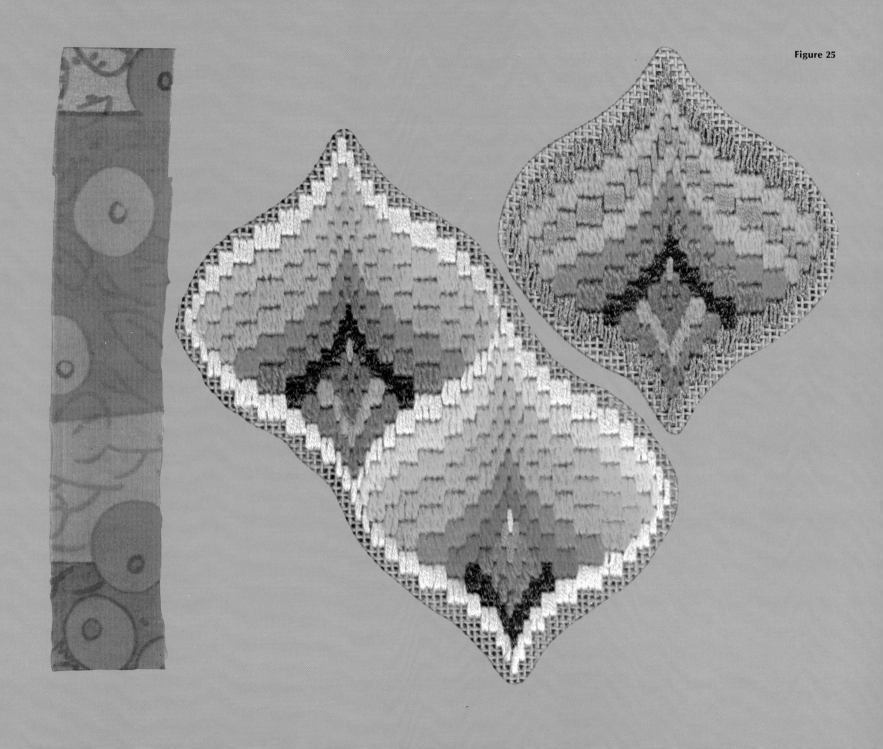

Figure 25

Fabrics, ribbon, and wallpapers can be adapted to needlework designs. Figure 25 shows the original fabric and three solutions for adapting the Pomegranate pattern. The fabric was analyzed and the following method was used to adapt the pattern.

Since some modern fabric forms are too rounded to duplicate in Bargello, a related but different form was used.

Color controls the coordination of a given pattern so the original fabric was studied, and its colors were matched with yarns using tints, tones, and shades. Even the vague accent colors were included. The pomegranate was worked with a gold outline, so that it became detached from the design and complemented other forms in the fabric. When a beige outline was used, it preserved the modern mood of the swatch.

Note was taken of the variety of colors in the fabric and rather than to repeat every color in one design motif, two different pomegranates were designed to be used in alternate repeats. Their colors were reversed, using darker centers in one and lighter centers in the other. The secondary rhythms that developed within the pomegranate were controlled with transition and contrast.

The most creative designs are those that come as direct responses to our emotions, intellects, .and interests. The elements discussed in this chapter are the tools to help you adapt your observations to the creation of a finished design. Develop the "seeing eye" and use the language of design, its elements, building blocks, and structural devices to bring into fruition your own ideas and impressions.

Bargello offers opportunities for infinite variety in design motifs without changing the method of stitchery. Employing color as the agent of change and using it in tandem with the other elements discussed in "Language of Design," remarkable patterns can be developed by altering a single motif. In the ten designs on the following pages, examples are given of possible ways to change rhythms, line directions, and interest areas within a single pattern. Explanations are provided to indicate how the emotional qualities of color work to abstract the reason of form. The basic outline of Fused Diamonds is always represented, and the resulting variations produce brilliant examples of color play, suggesting ways in which you can create new designs for your home.

Fused diamonds— ten variations

Using earth colors, the first pattern is based on the shading of a monochromatic harmony offset by contrast. The beige outline traces the pattern track and dominates the motif. Secondary patterns of diamonds are created as the shading varies from dark to light within the contrasting beige outline. Contrasts intensify each other, and the existing contrast between the beige outline and the darkest brown line adjacent to it starts the vibration of the secondary pattern path, directing the eye away from the bold outline and toward the center island where the rhythm rests. Using lighter beige tints in sufficient quantities creates a form forceful enough to arrest the rhythm of color in the center and lends repose to the pattern.

The two small diamonds worked in beige flanking the central forms act as accent to continue the vibration and redirect the eye to the pattern's track.

**FUSED DIAMONDS
NUMBER 1**

51 Fused diamonds—ten variations

Direct complements delicately shaded in the manner of tie-dyeing give the diamonds a misty, atmospheric effect reminiscent of a J. M. W. Turner painting.

The bold outline of the first pattern is subordinated by color gradation. It loses its identity as the palest pinks fuse in a rhythm of transition toward their fullest chroma of carmine red. No longer does the eye move around the defined track.

Light and color charge the atmosphere with lyric activity, and the pattern becomes a landscape of motion and mood anchored only by the dominant diamond forms that float in the shimmering field of color transition.

The shadowplay of color in transition continues in the shading of the diamonds, their segments worked in contrasting transitions of light to dark and dark to light. Green diamonds dominate.

FUSED DIAMONDS
NUMBER 2

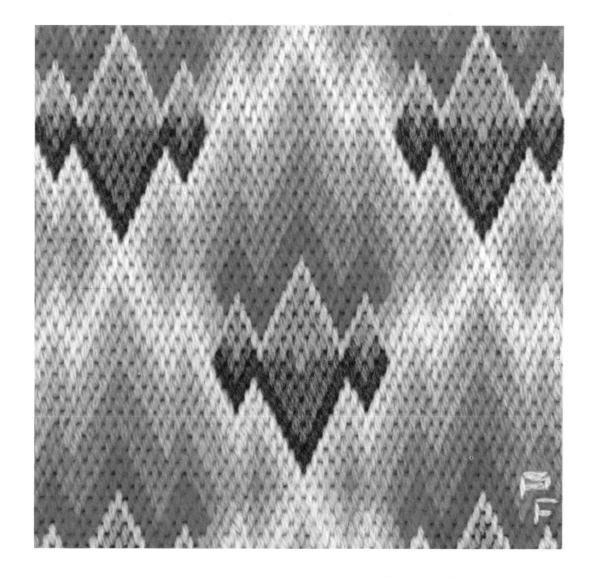

The outline returns and invites us to explore scale, the ladder of ratio and proportions. Vaguely we can see the shadowplay of the recessive diamond outlines, but the principal focus is on the beauty of the diamond form as its inner possibilities of related ratios and proportions are revealed. It is the contrasting dark line of green that sets the risers of the steps of the scale. The direction the dark line takes—its length, width, and repetitive cycle—delineates the scale of the pattern. If this line is repeated as a color chord separating the bands of shadings in the lower portion of the design as it does in Number 7, the scale and proportions are changed and the direction of the steps draws the eye horizontally across the canvas instead of toward the diamond forms.

Note that the contrasting colors in adjacent planes create borders that in turn form new shapes within these borders, creating interest as they play a part in the balance distribution of the background fields.

Note the difference in the clearly defined background field of Number 3 as opposed to the floating sensation of the field of Number 2.

Bold forms dramatically filled with contrasting colors from the vibrant palette of Gauguin comprise the statement of design in this variation. Hot pinks, orange, brilliant greens, mauve, and maroon call attention to the line direction and to the planes these line directions follow. Secondary shapes begin to dominate as they are worked in symmetrically balanced units. An ascending force is felt in the tepee-like forms produced by the bold outlines.

For the mind too fertile to be content with mere repetition, many new shapes now evolve, shapes shaded by spatial reflections in the background field. The basic planes are pulled apart like an accordion by the dominant forms of the green diamonds.

FUSED DIAMONDS
NUMBER 4

In this dramatic variation adapted from Aztec motifs, the bisected squares of the field are filled with warm analogous colors in an evenly balanced distribution. These squares compete with the diamond forms and point up the impact of their kinetic outlines. The strong movement of the jagged outline is controlled by the vertical and horizontal sectioning of the background. The squared background also draws attention to the forms in front of or behind the other shapes. The multidimensional quality of this composition invites the eye to follow its own impression of these overlays and the directions their rhythms can take.

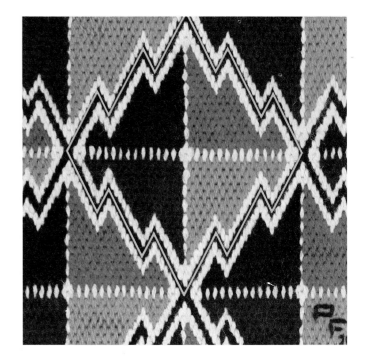

A quartet of diamonds segmented and worked in bold, contrasting argyle colors gives us a visual clue to the potentials of analytic cubism. Here the linear perspective of the original outline is lost. It now slumbers in the black against navy blue outlines, and our attention is directed toward the proportions of a diamond under conditions of extreme contrasts of light and dark and large and small. Note that the tiny white diamond, so diminutive in comparison with the other diamonds, supports the larger form in a chain of suspension giving the forms a floating feeling. The blue and white shapes appear as overlays on the red diamonds, and we are aware of an explosion of active shapes as our eye continues the optical destruction of the diamond forms.

Note that the sides of the white forms next to the red diamonds have greater depths to their edges, because the red against black lends greater contrast than navy blue against black on the other side.

At a distance from the design we see a large red X crossing in the center accented by a small white diamond. Now we realize the importance of the white highlights—they are the counterpoint of this pattern.

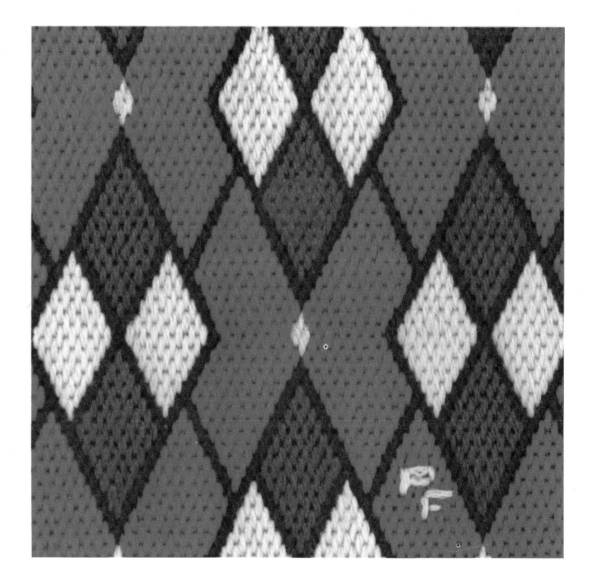

Brooding blues with textural highlights of silk bordered with contrasting black wool continue the game of optical illusion. The eye is directed away from the basic outline (it still is unchanged, but recessive to the superimposed diamond forms) to the rhythm of a horizontal plane. The color chords of highlighted pale blue and white diamonds interrupt the bold forms delineated in Numbers 1, 3, and 4 and change the direction of the rhythm. The sharp contrast between light forms and dark outlines creates a halo effect in the background and increases the dominance of the lighter forms.

The divided diamonds recede into the background, creating a lyrical tension as their motion is felt.

By using color combinations typical of Vasarely and encompassing the entire color wheel, further abstraction of forms is possible. The original shape of the large diamond is preserved in the muted white latticework that winds its way in and out of the segments. The basic outline, divided and redivided, appears to be completely subordinated to row after row of color swatches placed in yellow corridors. The magic mood of carnival color is disciplined to preserve the laws of "figure and ground" that our eyes are accustomed to. The diamonds retain their forms and are "thing-like" or "object-like" in impression. The orderly arrangement of their forms suggests a carpet of colored ribbons.

The bleeding of color that occurs when the stitches overlap in the divided diamonds aids in transition and blends the segments into a colorful whole much as panes in stained-glass windows. The opposite happens in Number 6 where white diamonds take over and become accents and highlights.

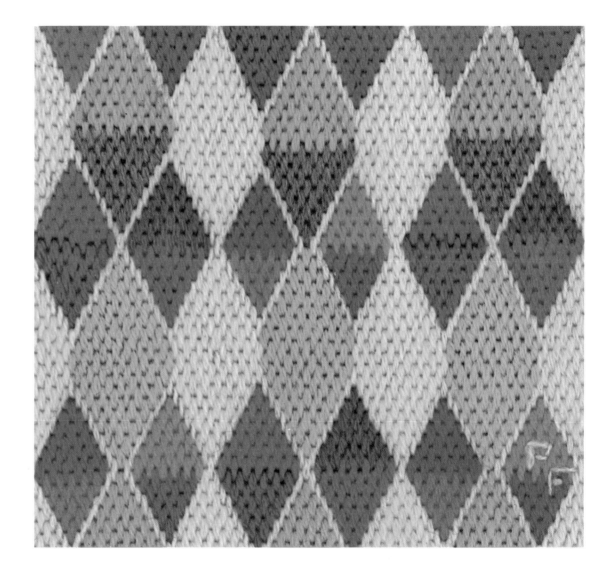

65 Fused diamonds—ten variations

Black and white neutrals are superimposed on each other in this variation which offers a dynamic study of line and shape in motion. The constant reversal of black and white forms lends a layered look to the design and creates this motion.

The tripled outline recedes from the alternating black and white rows producing an optical illusion of intaglio—it is as though the black diamonds are raised from the white field. They project into a forward plane and assume a dimensional quality. The eye is teased and tugged from diamond to diamond and lines appear to have thickness and thinness. The strong contrast of the neutrals is accompanied by a layered motion.

66

FUSED DIAMONDS
NUMBER 9

In the final variation, chevrons appear as the basic outline is partially abstracted into the white background field. New forms are developed as we become aware of the impact of color contrasts between the descending lines and the white field. These lines assume a dimensional quality and their downward movement becomes strong and dynamic, pulling the eye through the design. The emotional quality of color is monitored in this design by the reason of form. This form is reflected in the chevron shapes that lend stability to the pattern. Note the gradual transition of forms from small to large commencing at the peak of the chevron.

69 Fused diamonds—ten variations

NOTEBOOK OF PATTERNS

1 RIPPLING WAVE

The regular and simple rhythm of this beginner's pattern makes it particularly easy to combine with other fabrics in a room. A single color can be used with its shadings or a rainbow panorama can be developed with the use of analogous colors. Worked entirely in wool it takes on a country air; here bands of silk threads dress it up for more formal interiors.

The pattern is centered at top of canvas with block of 4 stitches and the first row is worked to right and left edges to set the pattern track. The rhythm is 1 stitch over 4 meshes with a step of 1.

2 RONDEL

The pattern track of Rippling Wave is reversed in its fifth row to form an eye-shaped niche which is worked in Whipped Spider Stitch.* Textural changes using wool, silk, and perle in alternating rows and in the niches formed by the mirror reverse of the pattern lend interest to the design.

The pattern is centered at top of canvas and is worked in a rhythm of 1 over 4 with a step of 1. The Bargello niche follows a rhythm of 1 over 2, 4, 6, and 8 (see graph).

* Occasionally patterns use stitches other than Bargello. Consult "Sources of Information" for recommended books to help extend your stitch vocabulary.

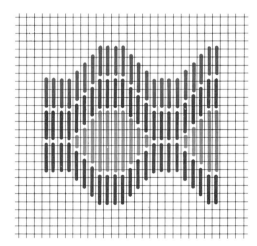

3 PINK PARFAIT

This delightful pattern in a monochromatic harmony offers opportunity for the use of the tints and shades of one color. The unbroken line pattern makes it suitable for large surfaces or for rounded surfaces such as lamp shades, and it adapts well to upholstery, fire screens, benches, pillows, and wastebaskets.

For a more dominant design, substitute a pale tint of green for the neutral gray in the interval area between color chords. Use orange, orange yellow, and brown with metallic threads and it becomes an Aztec motif.

Center peak at top of canvas and work to right and left edges. The rhythm is 1 over 4 with step 2.

4 BLUE JAY

The flashing colors of a bird on the wing are reflected in this pulsating pattern created by increasing the number of stitches to reach the peak. The valley at the top remains the same as in Pink Parfait (3), but the number of stitches is increased to 15 to reach the lower valley. Worked in orange to yellow orange with separation bands of black silk, Blue Jay takes on an Oriental quality and is effective in modern surroundings.

The rhythm is 1 over 4 with a step of 2. Center the twin peaks at top of canvas and work to right and left edges.

5 DENIM DAYS

Rough textures offer a simple rhythm using quick-working long stitches.

Start in the upper left-hand corner of the canvas and work downward diagonally with first color. The rhythm is 1 over 6 with a step of 1 for the first 3 stitches. There is an interval step of 5 down between each set of 3 stitches (see graph). The second row is worked in contrasting color under the first row of pattern track.

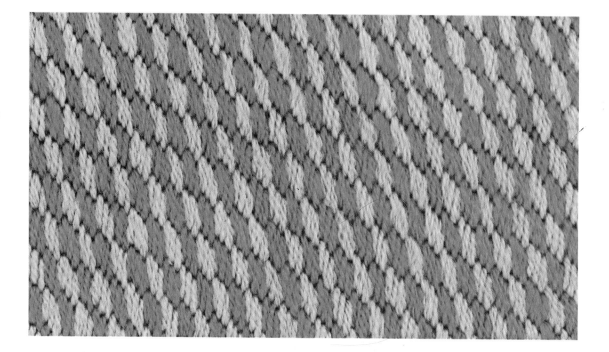

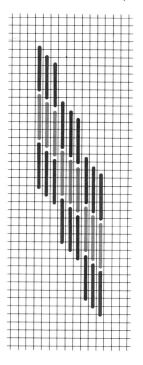

6 CORAL REEF

In Coral Reef stitch lengths vary in
successive rows to create an interesting
study of texture which is further
enhanced by the use of silk and
metallic threads with yarn. This pattern
is easy to work and its changing
stitch length relieves monotony.

Stitches vary in length for 3 rows and
are worked in a sequence of 1 over
4 in orange wool, 1 over 3 in orange
silk, and 1 over 2 in gold metallic
thread. The metallic thread is doubled.
The step is 1. Center the twin peaks
at top of canvas and work to right
and left edges.

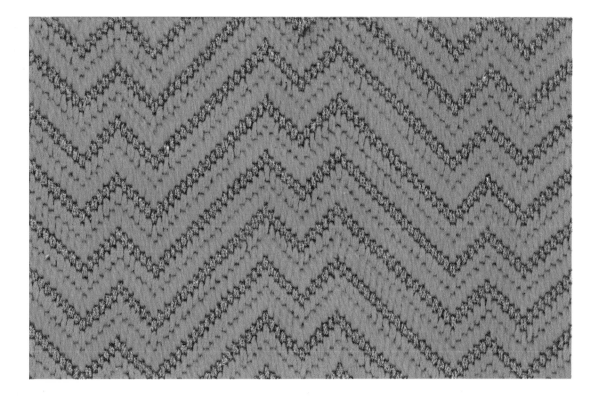

7 SEA NYMPH

Blues and greens of the frothy sea are
reflected in the colors of this design.
The irregular intervals between
color chords outlined with black key
set the rhythm of the pattern track. Its
continuous line makes it effective
for pieces subject to assemblage
such as vests, belts, boxes, and
handbags. Substituting metallic or
silk thread in some rows develops
a new pattern.

The rhythm is worked 1 over 4 with a
step of 2 in single stitches and blocks
of 4.

8 CHINESE JADE

Precious jade provides the color clue for this harmonious monochromatic color scheme, a simple beginner's pattern once the initial row has been established.

For dynamic variation, add separation bands of neutrals, white, black, or gray between repeats.

Start from the lower left-hand corner and work upward toward the right using a rhythm of 1 over 5 with a step of 2.

9 DEEP BOXES VARIATION

Abstract cubes play hide and seek
with shadows in this vividly contrasting
composition, offering a light and
dark perspective. Because the shading
is graded closely, the outline form
loses its impact and the pattern
becomes color controlled, making
the lower area deep and mysterious. By
reversing the colors the emphasis is
shifted to the border area and the
cube loses its depth.

Center the cube at top of canvas and
work white frames first using a rhythm
of 1 over 4 with a step of 2. Stitches
are worked in blocks of 2. The
repeat spins off from the side of
the pattern with the block of 2 stitches
bridging the repeats.

10 LOLLYPOP TREES
VARIATION

Brilliant Day-Glow colors abstract
this traditional pattern to subordinate
shape to color contrast. The familiar
lollypop trees become cushions of
layered, vibrant chroma intersected by
white standards.

Center the pattern at top of canvas.
The rhythm is 1 over 4 with a step
of 2 with the exception of the
2 stitches starting the fifth row at
the base of the tree. They are worked
over 2. Stitches are worked in blocks
of 2, 4, and 6. *Caution:* Watch
pattern track as you work each
row completely across canvas from
left to right since it is *important*
to leave 2 meshes void between
repeats. These voids will occur after
each tree, forming the trunks of
the tree above.

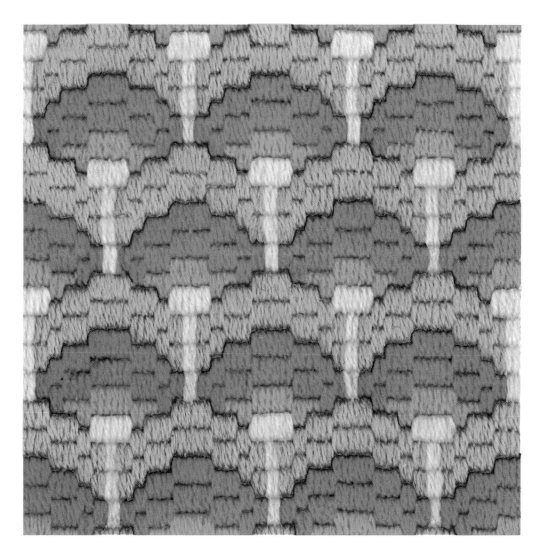

11 BASKET WEAVE VARIATION

Basket Weave takes on a carnival air with
this vibrant combination of paired analogous
harmonies. Worked in muted colors, particularly
beiges with browns, grays with red, or white
with blues or sepias, this pattern assumes the
traditional basket weave so suitable for English,
French, or Oriental interiors.

Start from the center bottom and work diagonally
the row of 8 stitches that has no segmented
bases. (Note that the other rows in this bottom
sequence have compensation stitches worked
over 2 to create a straight border.) Be sure that
the white crosses composed of 4 stitches over 4
are lined up evenly. They are the checkpoints
for this pattern. The rhythm is 1 over 4 with a
step of 2; all stitches are worked in blocks of
2 (see graph).

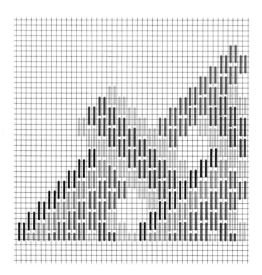

12 ALPINE SLOPES

A combination of knitting yarn, wool, and cotton perle is used to create a range of slopes and valleys highlighted with snowy white. Double the white bands and new color chords are created, changing the pattern.

Center the widest pronged peak at top of canvas. The rhythm is 1 over 3 with a step variation from 1 to 2. *Caution:* Study the pattern track and note these changes in step to prevent errors.

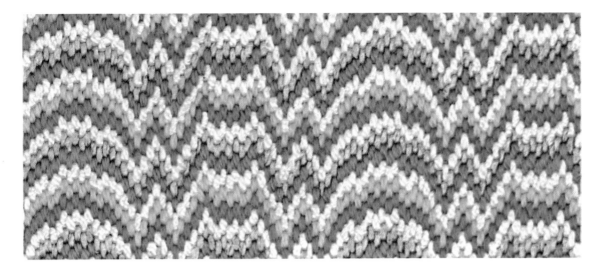

13 POMEGRANATE VARIATION

This classic pattern is given a modern
look with the stunning application
of red, white, gray, and black.
Shaded ribbons encircle the dramatic
central motif to create an exciting
three-dimensional study. Not for small
surfaces, this design is an instant
attention-getter when worked as a
vest, handbag, wastebasket, or pillow.

Center peak at top of canvas and
work white frames first in a gradation
of blocks of stitches stepped down
in the following units: 1, 1, 1,
2, 2, 3, 4, 3, 2, 2, 1, 1, 1, using a
rhythm of 1 over 4 with a step of 2.

14 CLOISTERS

Cloisters, which uses black bands between the color chords, is an adaptation of the Rippling Wave (1). The abstracted pillars create perspective corridors highlighted with the brilliant red accent stitches.

Center pattern at top of canvas and, starting with a white row, work through grays to black. The rhythm is 1 over 4 with a step of 1.

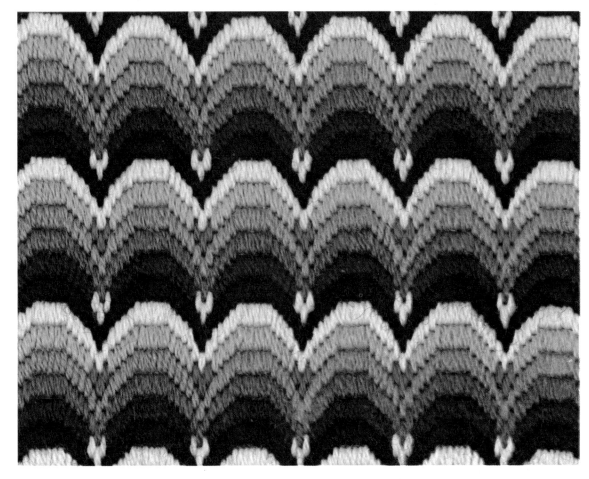

15 ROSE WINDOW

The vibrant colors of a stained-glass window are captured in this adaptation of *opus Anglicanum*. A variation of the traditional pomegranate form, it is also known as Peacock Eye because of its use in needlework to accent the feathers of this exotic bird. Rose Window is particularly adaptable to design changes.

Center the pattern on the canvas and work the frames first. To fill the frames, work around from the center top in the same rhythm as the frame until the center eye stitches are reached. *Caution:* Center stitches share a mesh. Rhythm is 1 over 4 with a step of 2. Blocks step down in the following units: 1, 1, 1, 3, 3, 3, 1, 1, 1.

16 PERSIAN GARDEN

This dainty interval repeat has the delicate quality of a Persian print. The concept of a void column between repeats used in Lollypop Trees (**10**) is employed here.

The fuchsia frames forming the background grill are worked first in a rhythm of 1 over 4 with a step of 1, except for the first stitch of the lower part of frame which steps down 3. The column, marked *X* on graph, is left open and filled in later with the stem.

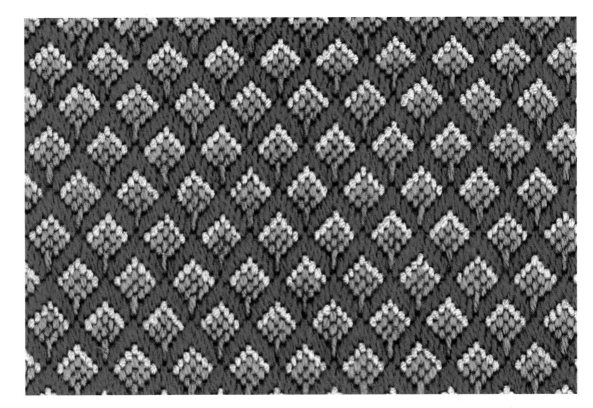

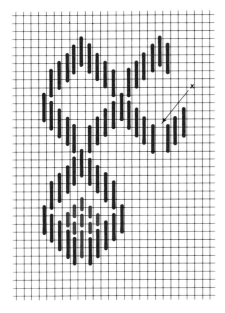

17 PERSIAN GRILL

The beautiful grillwork of Persia comes to life in this complementary harmony using blue and orange. The small repeat makes it practical for belts and handbags, trinket boxes, address books, and doll furniture.

Center the pattern in the middle of the canvas and work the frames of the interval repeats first. The rhythm is 1 over 4 with a step of 2. Blocks of stitches vary in number in the repeats and stitches frequently share meshes. *Caution:* Work the pattern track on a doodle cloth first to master the repeat, because the centers of the motifs vary in their filler stitches.

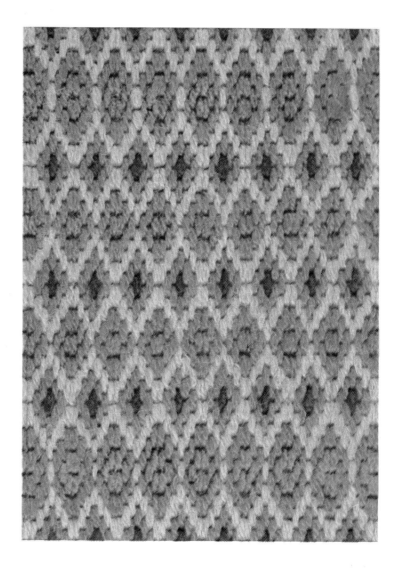

18 HERB GARDEN

This pattern has a flexible identity, working well with many interiors. A striking effect is achieved working one repeat in tints and tones of blue and the next entirely in white.

Start the middle stitch of the peak in the center of the canvas, working to left and right edges.
A green row is worked first, followed by a white one. Another green row starts the pattern repeat.
In the first row of green, watch for the void between the 2 sequences marked V on graph.
This void will be filled with a white stitch sharing a mesh with another white stitch in the row below (see X on graph).

Green rows are worked first, 1 stitch over 4 with exception of center stitch of 1 over 3.
White row is worked 1 stitch over 2 with exception of middle peak over 3. The stitch worked in the void column is 1 over 6. All steps are 1.

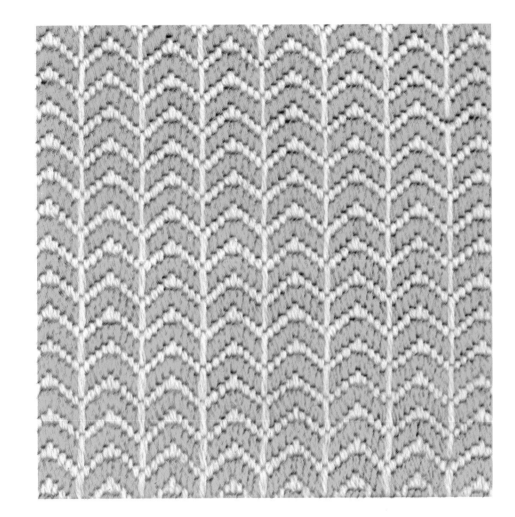

19 PASTILLES

In this pattern for intermediate stitchers, careful counting is needed to establish the spools.
Once they are set, the centers are easily mastered.

The spools are worked first with the block of 4 stitches over 5 meshes centered 4 rows under top of canvas. There are 25 meshes needed across the repeat. All stitches have a step of 1 with the exception of the longest stitch in the spool which is worked over 11 meshes with a step of 4 down.

The center motif is 1 over 3, 5, 7, 9 (see graph).

Variations for the centers can be devised by alternating colors, by working canvas stitches such as Continental or Whipped Spider, or by substituting floral motifs.

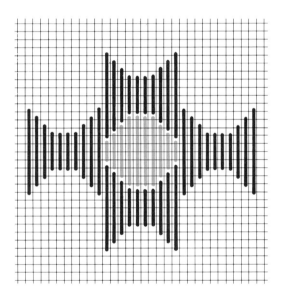

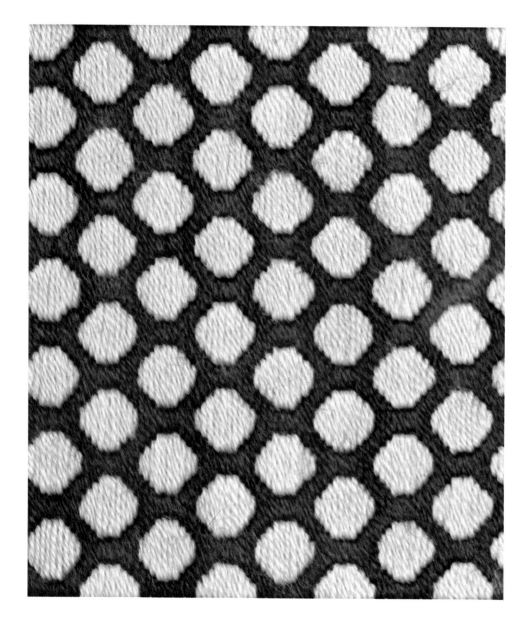

The repeated motif of parallelograms worked in reverse in alternating rows gives the impression of sculptured sticks. The black background lends depth to the composition. The same pattern with a slight variation is used as a background in Family Tree (**31**), worked in a combination of wool and silk. Eye-catching bracelets, watchbands, or cigarette boxes can be made using tobacco brown and beige colors. To make the pattern more suitable for articles designed for wear, work the sticks horizontally, with the 2 center stitches of each stick in another color.

The rhythm is 1 over 8 with a step of 1. Work up from bottom of canvas. The key to the repeat lies in starting the first stitch of the second row of parallelograms over the middle stitch of the previous row (see *X* on graph).

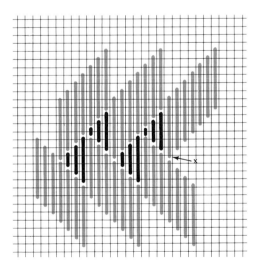

The freshness of an English garden is reflected in this charming pattern with its small-scaled segments. An unusual mosaic pattern develops when it is worked in tortoiseshell tans and brown combining silk with wool.

Work dark green stitches first in a rhythm of 1 over 4 with a step of 1. Each stitch skips a mesh. Void columns are then filled with light green wool, each stitch over 2 sharing a mesh.

The lavender motifs are worked last in a rhythm of 1 over 2, over 4, over 6, with exception of 2 center stitches which are 1 over 4 sharing a mesh.

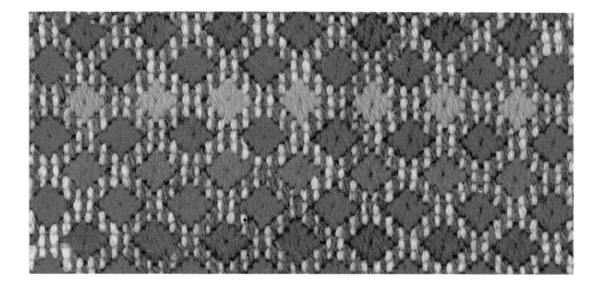

22 CINNEBAR

The beauty of Oriental enamel work
is echoed in this pattern with its
exquisite detail. Note how the interval
repeats develop secondary patterns
in their niches.

Work all frames first. (The bottom
row is left with unfinished frames
to aid in mastering the pattern track.)
Center the block of 5 stitches
over 4 at top of canvas. From this
block work wings composed of 3
stitches: 1 over 8 with a step of 2, over
5 with a step.of 2, and over 6 with
a step of 4 to a peak; reverse and
repeat the unit to valley. Turn pattern
and work same stitches. This wing
is worked on either side of the block
of 5 central stitches. The repeat below
spins off from it and another block
of 5 stitches is worked between
those wings. The center is worked in
multicolored filler stitches using
silk thread. The stitches are of a
different length but the step is over 1
with the exception of the center
crosses. Stitches frequently share
meshes to change directions;
this pattern should be worked first
on a doodle canvas to master
its complexities.

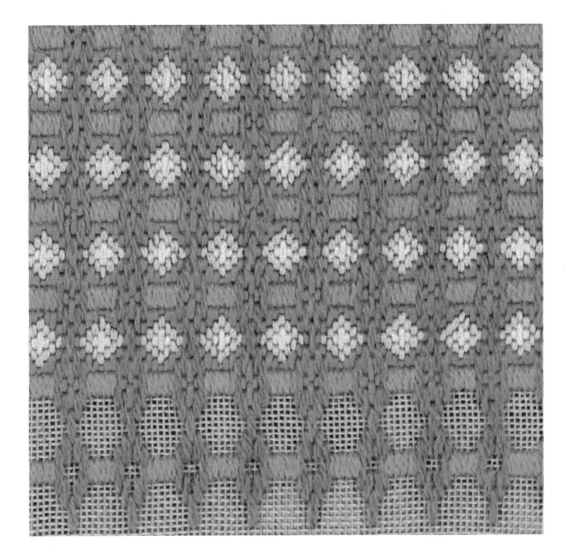

The feather adapts itself through textures and alternating repeats in this intermediate pattern which involves vertical and horizontal mesh sharing.

The feathers can be separated with vanes of Continental or with upright Gobelin Stitches in contrasting silk textures. A green silk feather intersected with rows of black produces an Empire feeling.

Center on bottom of canvas and work upright to the left as shown on graph. All stitches share a mesh to change direction and the rhythm is 1 over 4 with a step of 1. The intersections of the meshes are couched diagonally with a stitch of 1 over 5. Compensation stitches to complete fragmented segments of the pattern are worked last to a straight border.

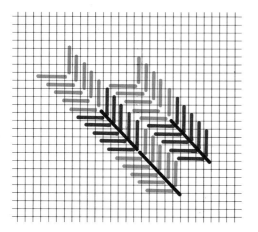

24 FRENCH RIBBON

This small repeat is a good vehicle for problem pieces because its diagonal pattern adapts well to areas of unequal proportions. Human hair is used for the silver stitches connecting the pink buds. Synthetic or real hair is an excellent substitute for metallic threads because it won't crack or fray and is stronger than most fibers. If necessary to dye the hair silver, spray with waterproof color, allow to dry, and brush with clear nail polish to fuse ends and give it substance. Use short strands and gauge width by the size of the mesh to be covered.

The rhythm is 1 over 4 with a step of 2. The buds are formed with a simple grounding. Start the pattern at the lower left-hand corner and work upward. This pattern should be worked on a stretcher.

25 FRENCH FLOWER BASKETS

Pale pinks, blues, and greens with mauve accent form the delicate color harmonies for the iris worked in a detached repeat. Violets, roses, daffodils, or fruit can be substituted for the iris flower in the basket. In Bay Scallops (**26**) on facing page, a complex shell design is developed using the basic outline.

If contrasting stitches of Continental are worked for the background of the basket, greater depth is created for the composition. For example, see Blue Cymbidium (**47**). The design takes on a Victorian quality if the basket is worked in silver thread with the flowers in silk against wool.

There are 44 meshes vertically in the basket and the design should be started 22 meshes above center of canvas with the block of 9 stitches that form the center top of the basket handle. Stitches outlining basket are 1 over 4 with a step of 2. Iris stitches vary 1 over 1, 2, or 4, and background consists of even rows of 1 over 2.

Stitches frequently share a mesh and there are thicks and thins in the blocks of stitches.

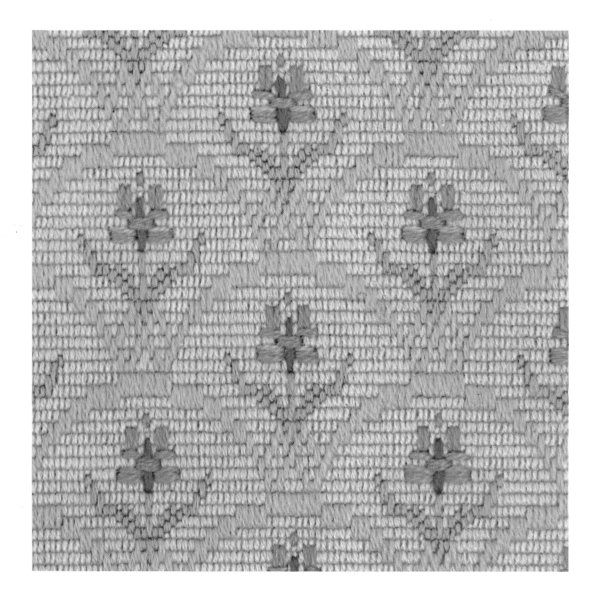

The remarkable contours of the seashell have been used for design motifs since man's first efforts to duplicate nature's wonders. A bay scallop was used to provide the form for this pattern.

The design can be worked in a traditional form repeat, or abstracted as in the sample shown. The pattern has a reciprocal relationship with Oriental-scale patterns, and once you have mastered the repeat, Oriental motifs can be devised.

Start with block of 9 stitches at the top of shell, centering them in the middle of canvas. Work outline first in a rhythm of 1 over 4 with a step of 2. Work the ridges of the shell in a contrasting color and follow the outline rhythm, filling the shell in graded colors. The pattern spins its repeat from the 9 stitches. Check the pattern frequently to be certain the matching blocks of stitches in the outline are directly opposite each other.

27 REFLECTIONS VARIATION

Hungarian Point in a rhapsody of color is worked in this pattern which is highlighted by a background of simple groundings.

The rhythm is a combination of 2 stitches each over 6, and 2 stitches each over 2.

Start with the highest peak in center of canvas and work to right and left borders to establish 1 row of the pattern track. Work subsequent rows under this first row using the following color sequence:

5 rows of rust, dark to light
2 rows of beige silk
6 rows of blue, light to dark
2 rows of beige silk
2 rows of yellow
Follow with blues

The background consists of an interval of beige silk worked in a grounding pattern of 1 over 2, 4, 6, 4, 2.

Keep a color-sequence chart handy and check your pattern frequently for errors.

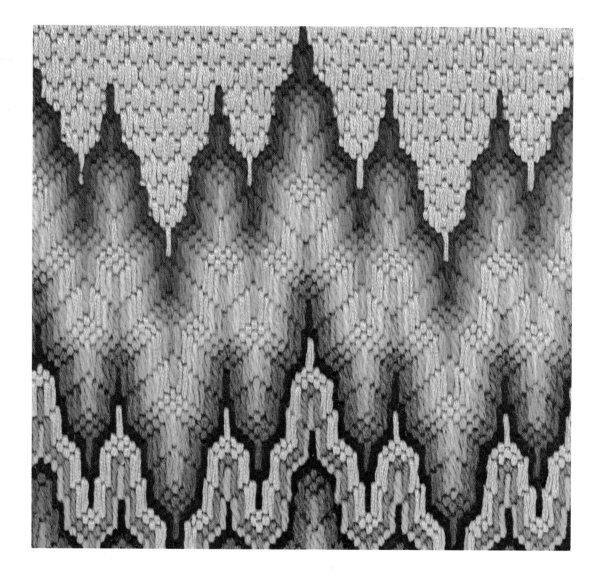

Jute twine and a large-eyed needle were used to work this Hungarian Point adaptation on Penelope rug canvas (5 meshes to inch).

Jute twine does not twist or require disciplined guidance to shape its stitches, and this pattern is excellent for junior projects of tote bags, athletic carry-alls, placemats, or purses.

The design can also be worked on mono-canvas No. 16 with wool, silk, or metallic threads. It is particularly lovely in apricot, browns, silver, and gold. See, for example, Aubusson Symphony (**41**).

The rhythm is 1 over 6 and 3 over 2 with a step of 1.

There are 54 meshes from top to bottom. Locate the center of the canvas and count up 27 stitches from the center point and place the first stitch 1 over 6 for top of frame. Work all frames first, checking to be sure that opposite sides match. The center of the design repeats the rhythm of the frame, and stitches are fragmented to fit the niche. The repeat is spun off from the side of the frame at the middle long stitch.

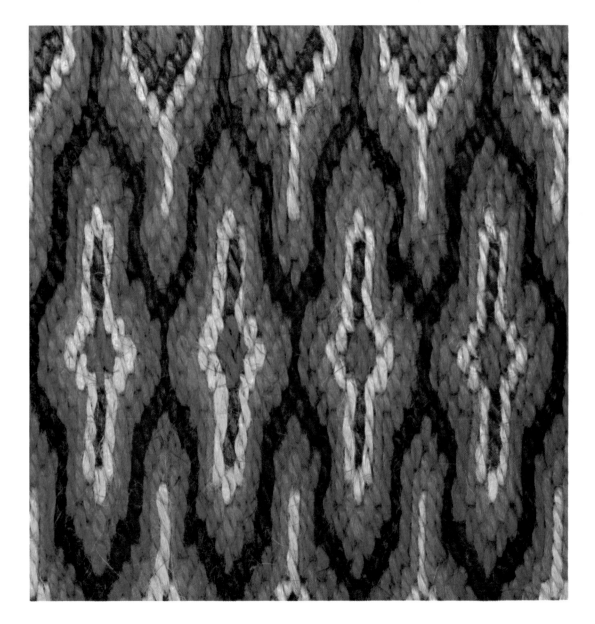

29 STRAWBERRY FIELDS

Crimson silky strawberries tucked in gold metallic frames form a delicate pattern for a dainty surface.

Work the frames first in alternate blocks starting at the center top with a block of 3 stitches,* a block of 2, 2, 1, 1 then reverse, working downward to complete berry.

The alternate berry has a rhythm starting at the top of 1 working down 1, 2, 2, 3 and reversing to return to top.

The key lies in joining frames: 2 blocks of 3 stitches share meshes.

The frames are filled with the same rhythm, worked to the outside track.

* Note that metallic threads are always doubled.

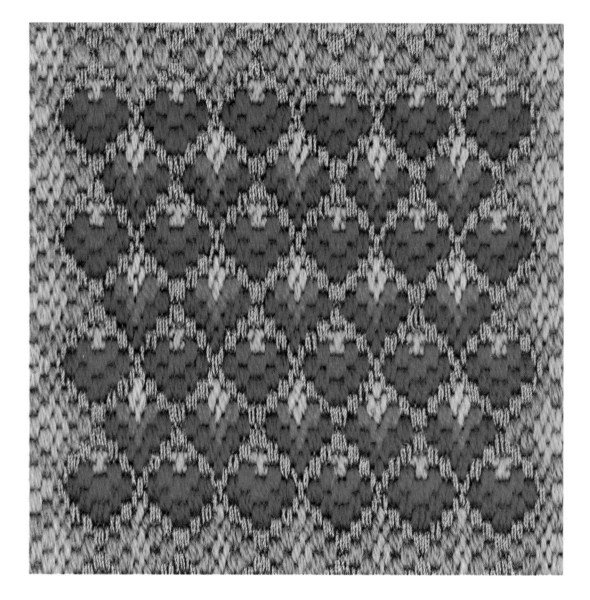

Maple sugar, spruce trees, and red berries provide the color key for Country Cousins. Color chords of monochromatic harmonies in maple and honey shades are separated by spruce-green bands.

The same band can be worked with wheat, grapes, apples, or insects in the niches. The design assumes a formal feeling when worked in brilliant blues and greens with a white or gray silk center for the niche.

Start pattern in center of canvas and work to right and left edges. The rhythm is 1 over 6 with a step of 3. All stitches are worked in blocks of 2. The diamond-shaped niches are worked with a motif of mistletoe entwined on a branch.

After the rows are worked, a horizontal stitch in bright red silk is worked in a running stitch across the blocks of 2 stitches.

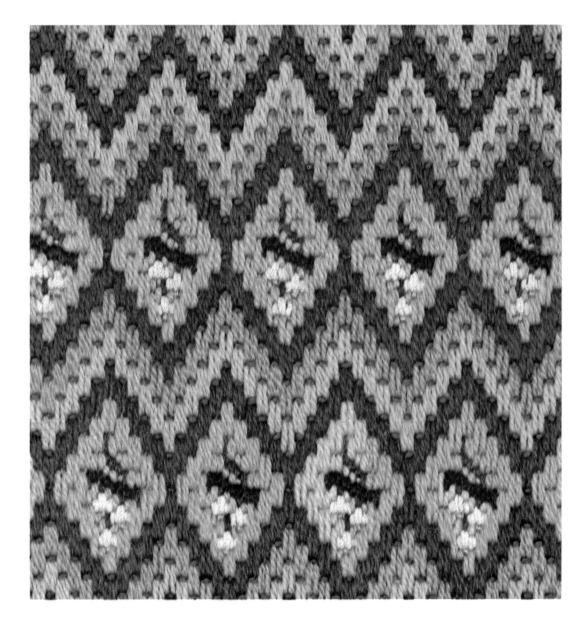

31 FAMILY TREE

Grounding units are pyramided into a family tree which can be worked as a decorative motif as shown or used to record family names in the void areas. These areas can be enlarged by working in blocks of 3, 4, and 6 stitches according to the area needed to record the names. Interesting color substitutions are brown trunk, dark blue groundings, and orange-shaded letters against a lighter blue background.

The rhythm is 1 over 4 with a step of 2. All stitches are in blocks of 2 except the trunk. Work outline first.

A grounding repeat, the same one used in Family Tree (**31**), is employed as an alternate repeat in Art Nouveau. This pattern also works beautifully in an alternating repeat with shaded centers. Flower forms may be substituted from Country Cousins (**30**) and French Ribbon (**24**).

Center the peak stitch in middle of top of canvas and work all frames first. They are worked in blocks of 2 stitches, each over 4 with a step of 2. The flowers are worked in espalier groupings, the background color setting the pattern in relief or absorbing it into an impression. The stems of the flowers continue upward through the latticework in alternating repeats.

33 BYZANTINE

Exotic enamels were the inspiration for this dainty pattern. Its small scale makes it adaptable for belts, handbags, or eyeglass cases.

Complete the gold metallic outline stitches first, working diagonally in a rhythm of 1 over 2 with a step of 1. The areas between the gold boxes formed in the outline stitches are then filled with stitches in tints and shades of greens and violets. The small-diamond boxes are filled last with lilac silk in a rhythm of 1 over 2 with a step of 1.

This unusual repeat pattern is adaptable to modern as well as period decor, and it is especially interesting for bridge chairs because of its spadelike form.

Starting at the top of canvas 5 stitches from the center, work the black outline first in a rhythm of 1 over 4 and 1 over 2 with a step of 1 (see graph).

In this pattern the gold metallic threads are worked *after* the black outline frame is set. Fill the remainder of the design with long and short stitches in a rhythm of 1 over 4 and 1 over 2, with a step of 1.

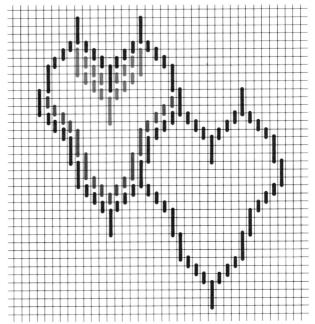

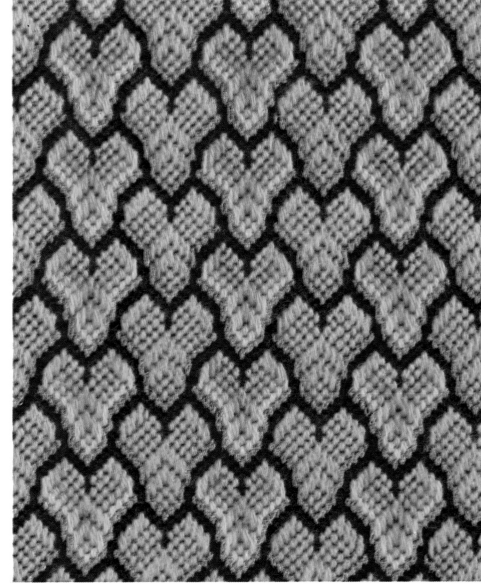

Austrian Plissé uses detached
flowers and butterflies between
bands of ribbons, and its simple wave-
patterned background provides a
curtained movement.

The pattern is worked out on graph
paper first with the grid carefully
counted to center the motifs. The
width of the separation bands of
ribbon should be varied according
to the scale of the piece the
pattern covers.

Work the ribbon bands first in a
rhythm of 1 over 4. The background
rhythm is 1 over 2 with a step of 1. The
background pattern can be reversed
to achieve a swag effect.

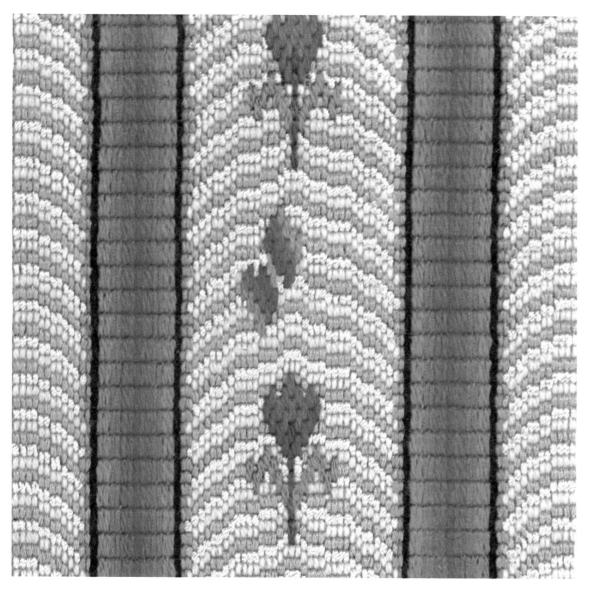

This fantasy piece is created with combinations of small design devices worked in and around a central geometric form. The frame for the flower is a segment of an interval repeat pattern. The Pomegranate (**13**), carnation, and most diamond-shaped patterns can be adapted to frame motifs.

Work the geometric frame first, the center flower and butterflies, then the ribbons connecting to the central motif.

The background of the pattern simulates a moiré fabric and is worked in 1 over 4 and 1 over 2 in blocks of 6 stitches (see graph). It is best worked from the outside in as a border, completing one turn around the square to set the corner turn before working toward the center. The background of the central motif is worked in Brick Stitch.

This pattern is best worked on graph paper first to place the motifs accurately.

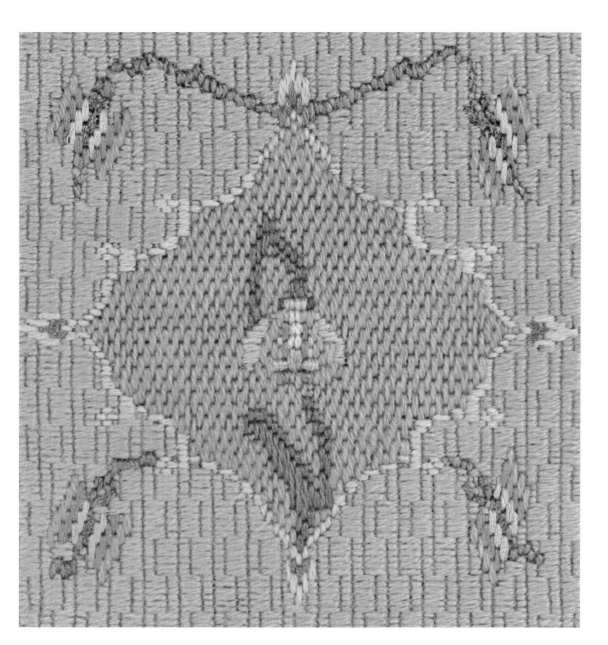

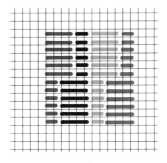

This modern design reverses the repeat in ribbon units. It is stunning for accent pillows, especially if they are worked in dynamic colors. Equally good for shoulder bags, belts, suspenders, or fishing-rod cases it can be worked in red, white, and blue or coral, aqua, white, and leather tan.

This pattern should be drawn on graph paper first to establish the number of ribbon repeats. Space the repeats an equal distance apart on graph paper and plan to work additional background color between ribbon strips. *Note:* Because ribbon strips are reversed, background areas become more important. Center the motif in units of 2 repeats.

Stitches are worked vertically and horizontally with varying steps and stitch lengths (see graph).

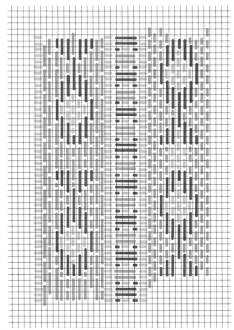

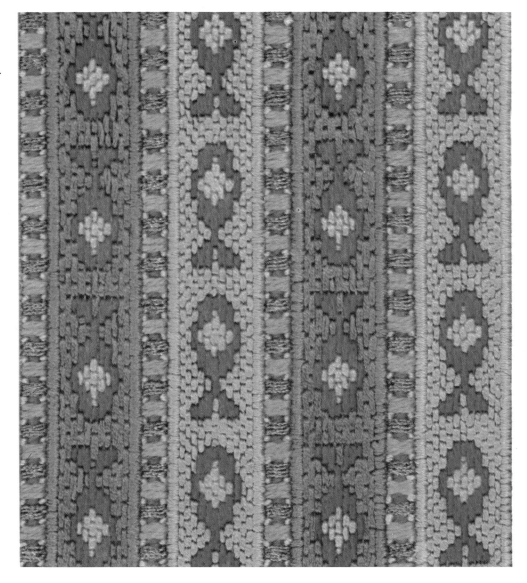

Strawberries, hearts, and marigolds share intervals with hex signs in this familiar motif. Ribbon compositions like Pennsylvania Dutch and Austrian Plissé (35) offer staging areas for nostalgic samplers.

In all ribbon patterns draw the design first on graph paper, counting the meshes carefully to scale them to the area you wish to cover.

Work the marigold first. The marigold starts with a center placement of 1 Cross Stitch over 5 meshes. From the sides of the cross, 2 stitches are worked over 3 sharing meshes. The corner stitches repeat this rhythm for 2 rounds. The other stitches in the flower are over 1, over 2, over 3. The stem is a combination of 1 over 2 and 1 over 3, with a step of 1. Note that the flowers slightly differ as they turn left and right profiles.

The ribbons are worked in Brick Stitch 1 over 4 with the exception of the white fringe which is 1 over 2.

In this pattern for advanced stitchers, rhythm works with color to produce a striking design. Worked entirely in silk, the change of rhythm and coordination of color give the illusion of direction change. Analogous harmonies of green to yellow green are offset by purple tints and tones shadowed by intervals of dark beige. The background of light beige sharpens the outline of the central motif and presents an interesting study in texture.

Center tallest peaks at top of canvas and work darkest shade first to establish pattern track. The rhythm is 1 over 6 with a step of 5 down.

The dark beige outline sets the pattern track for the background, worked in a rhythm of 1 over 6 with a step of 1 in increasing blocks. Note that the background peak starts its descent over the base of the turret.

For the repeat, reverse left and right motifs to form alternating turrets and spires. (Note that two stitches will form the spire peak.)

This pattern is worked on 18-mesh ecru canvas. It should not be worked in silk unless this difficult medium has been thoroughly mastered.

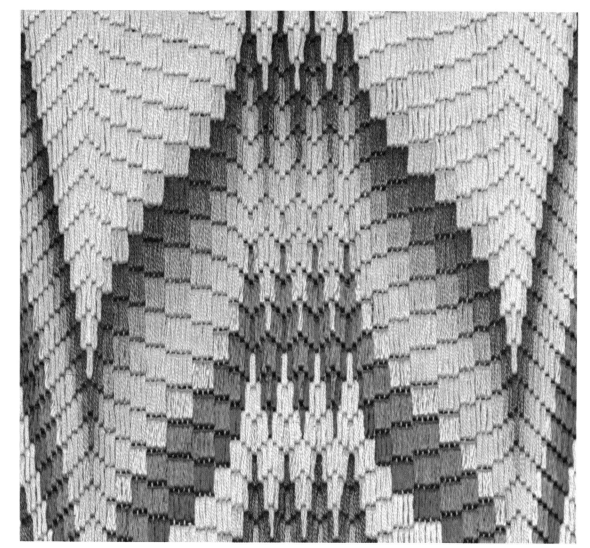

This dramatic adaptation of Hungarian Point worked in a triadic harmony combines successfully all the elements of good design. The colors flow into the repeat of the pattern, it expresses motion with repose, and the long and short stitches in the rhythm give depth to the brocaded textures.

Color sequence plays an important part in the pattern development. The repeats are worked in 4 colors: green, yellow, rose, and blue, highlighted by a row of ecru silk.

Center the tallest peak in the middle of the canvas and work to the right and left edges.

The rhythm is 1 long stitch over 6 meshes followed by 4 short stitches over 2 meshes with a step of 1.

This exquisite pattern uses cotton, wool, silk, and metallic to vary its theme, and features changing motifs in each medallion as well as an unusual background.

To set the pattern   Quarter the canvas by drawing guidelines. Count 20 meshes from center and work first long stitch over 6 upward followed by 4 stitches over 2 with a step down of 1.

Work 4 repeats in plateaus to a single peak before starting down to complete the 4 repeats ending in a valley of 1 long stitch. This is the rhythm which is repeated in plateaus and peaks worked in long and short stitches across the canvas.

Return to starting stitch, skip the 2 canvas meshes below, and repeat the pattern sequence working downward. This will form medallions or niches across the canvas which are left void until the rest of the pattern and the background are worked. Continue the pattern repeat on both sides of the niches until the borders are reached. Compensation stitches are worked in the open meshes when the next row is begun.

Niche motifs   The center niche is monogrammed in delicately shaded period initials with a background of Continental.

Return to adjoining niches and work voids in a rhythm of 1 over 6 followed by 4 over 2, working inside border of niche in silver

metallic thread. Continue working inside niche decreasing stitches to fit the area, repeating pattern track.

Note the sequence of colors listed below and follow it carefully.
   1 row perle
   4 rows antique gold wool, shading from *light* to *dark*
   1 row perle
   1 row peach silk
   3 rows peach wool
   1 row perle
   4 rows beige silk, shading from *light* to *dark*
   1 row gold metallic
   1 row silver metallic
   1 row perle

Background   The background is worked in voids between the pattern track and border of canvas using silk and gold metallic threads in a rhythm of 1 over 2, over 4, over 6, over 4, over 2. Compensation stitches between grounding pattern and last row of long and short rhythm are worked in gold metallic to fill the remaining voids.

Caution: It is important to know the pattern track before starting to work because the materials are expensive and should not be reused if ripped out.

42 FLORENTINE SIGNETS

Renaissance opulence is captured in this elegant pattern so suitable for trinket boxes, handbags, or accent pillows. It is worked entirely in metallic and silk threads.

Substitutions for the metallic and silk threads change the character of the design. White wool used with blue greens, moss rose, and yellow ocher or jungle green, tropic gold, hibiscus pinks, and orchid with black frames produce a striking modern adaptation.

Complete all frames first; stitches are worked horizontally 1 over 2. Follow with inner rows of olive and yellow silk.

The signet centers are made of a block of 6 stitches of 1 over 4 flanked by single stitches of 1 over 2. Note that the clusters of signets have alternate groupings.

The metallic signets are worked with single strands in a Brick Stitch of 1 over 2.

Caution: Ecru canvas is essential because the metallic threads do not cover the background entirely and the canvas shows through as a filigree.

Nature lends forms for this ribbon repeat which combines simple Bargello stitches with elegant materials to produce a design that is effective as an overall pattern or a border.

Divide the canvas into equal parts and center a vine in each segment. (There are 25 meshes between outside edges of grapes.) Begin stitches at bottom of canvas and work upward and sideways in a rhythm of 1 over 2 with a step of 1. The grapes spin off by sharing 2 meshes under the vines.

As in Florentine Signets (**42**), on facing page, backgrounds are worked in Brick Stitch, using single strands of gold metallic thread. Ecru canvas must be used.

44 QUILTING BEE

This colorful pattern has a sculptured look to its gay little squares. The random color variations suggest Op Art. Because of the length of the stitch (1 over 8), Quilting Bee is not recommended for surfaces that are in constant use. Try it for accent pillows, doll furniture, or under glass-topped tables.

Center the pattern at top of canvas. The squares are worked in 4 triangles, 2 horizontal and 2 vertical, with stitches 1 over 8, over 6, over 4, over 2, with a blue stitch in the center to cover the joint of the stitches. Five colors are used ranging from shocking pink to vermilion.

Caution: This pattern should be worked on a stretcher to keep the tension even, since the stitches change directions.

45 CONFETTI PATCHWORK

As in Quilting Bee (**44**) color control is the keynote here. A potpourri of pattern develops when a simple grounding is worked in similar textures but with different colors.

Divide the canvas into 4 equal parts and center the pattern on intersecting lines, working repeats from this center placement.

Blocks are worked in 5 rows of confetti dots, 7 in a row, to create a square.

The groundings are worked in 2 colors in a pattern track of 1 over 4, 2 over 6, 1 over 4. Note that 2 meshes are skipped between the groundings.

The skipped meshes between dots are worked last with horizontal stitches threaded under the confetti dots. Starting from left with a long thread work toward right, weaving the thread under the dots.

Caution: Watch that the dots on the vertical center line are worked in 2 colors equally divided.

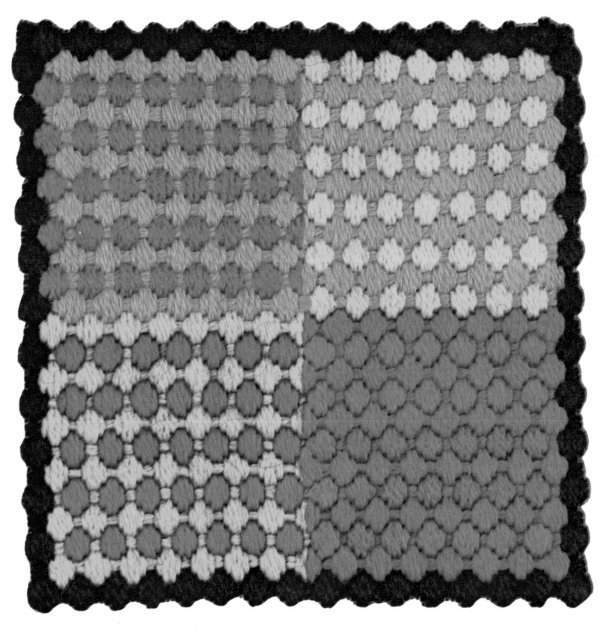

In this pattern, groundings are grouped about a center segment to form a flower.

Start at the top of your canvas with the 4 longest stitches, each over 10, centered. Note that the colors alternate. Complete the grounding with stitches worked vertically over 8, over 6, over 4 flanking the center placement of 4 stitches over 10. Sharing a mesh with the stitch over 4 and working horizontally, place a stitch over 4 in contrasting color. From this point repeat the pattern track working horizontally and sharing meshes with stitches of the first pattern track where they are adjacent. The 2 long stitches at the center are adjacent to void meshes which are worked last.

The pattern track is repeated in the next 2 segments that match in opposite repeat. The spin off for the alternate grounding starts from the shortest stitch of the petal segment and is worked in an opposite direction sharing a mesh. Note that the center segments of the flowers are worked in blocks of 4 stitches over 2. The segment of background between flowers is worked in blocks of 3 stitches over 3.

Four pomegranate motifs are combined in a clover leaf pattern to form a cymbidium orchid. The pattern—a textural study using wool, silk, and metallic threads—is worked from the center out. Two vertical stitches over 6 share a mesh in the center. Two horizontal stitches over 5 *appear* to intersect vertical stitches but actually do not (see *X* on graph). From this placement, stitches 1 over 4 with a step of 2 are worked in the Pomegranate pattern (**13**). The center voids and background are worked in Continental.

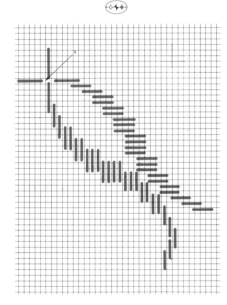

Using color transition as a vehicle, form bursts
forth in a symphony of closely related analogous
harmonies for this stunning composite of vertical,
horizontal, and diagonal stitches. The center
cross is worked with silk; the border of compensation stitches is in gold metallic threads.

Locate the center of the canvas and work 4 stitches
to form center cross. Each stitch is over 6 meshes
and shares a mesh to change direction. Next,
work chevrons of 11 stitches each within points of
4-sided star, using analogous colors. Continue
adding chevrons until you reach border. The
corridors between chevrons are then couched with
diagonal stitches as in Feather Vanes (**23**)
(see graph).

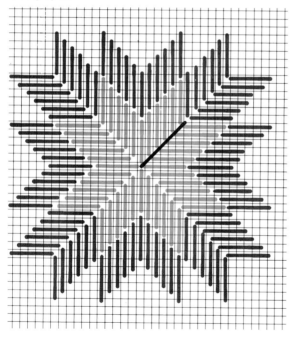

The iridescent colors of Tiffany glassware are captured in this composite design. It can be worked in repeat, centered in a background of groundings as shown, or extended like Star Bright (**52**). Both motifs are beautiful on a lamp shade, for a trinket boxtop, desk accessory set, or evening bag. Textures used are wool and silk.

The pattern is worked from the center placement of 4 stitches, each over 2. Stitches 1 over 3 share corner meshes to enlarge the center. The fan-shaped wings are 1 over 6 with a step of 1, graduating to 1 over 2 at the ends. Compensation stitches are used between the fans and central placement.

This pattern is an excellent example of dominance at work as the colorful centers lend activity to the pattern. The frame of Pastilles (**19**) was adapted to a niche for the medallion used as the center device.* Alternating rows of silk and wool medallions give the composition its unique texture.

Work the frames first adding one extra stitch in the center of the frame to give an uneven number of meshes to accommodate the medallion. Work medallion from the center out, placing the star first. Note that the star is formed by one stitch crossing over the other.

* See graph on page 90 for stitch count of frame. Note that 5 stitches are used across top and bottom of medallions instead of 4 as shown on graph.

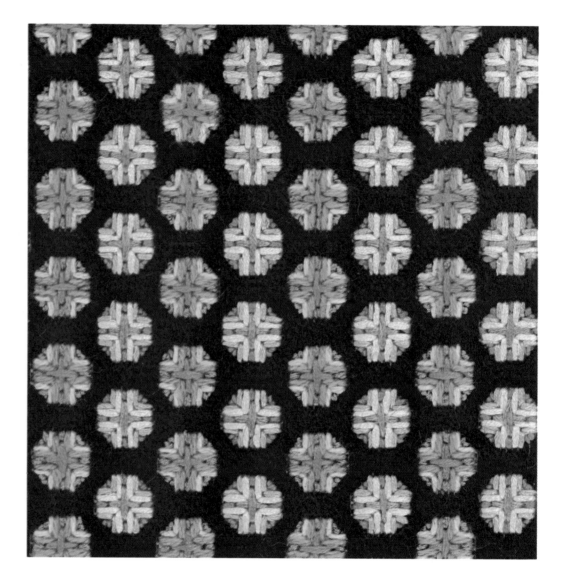

51 PINWHEELS

Fuchsia and mauve wool lend accent to this colorful pattern. Secondary patterns develop between the pinwheels, and offer numerous opportunities to vary the motif. They can be worked using tints as shown or in contrasting harmonies. Silver, white, and gray pinwheels, with black and red secondary areas make a dynamic pattern. To make a Bargello composite, extend the points of the star to the borders and fill in the voids with segments of the points.

Center a pinwheel in the middle of the canvas, working 4 stitches from the center. The rhythm is 1 over 4 with a step of 1 worked horizontally and vertically sharing a mesh to change direction. The pinwheel points are worked at right angles in the niches formed by the first 4 stitches (see graph).

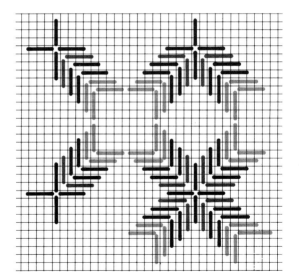

An exquisite star develops from this Bargello composite which uses a medley of pinks, reds, and greens worked in wool and mercerized cotton.

The pattern is started from the center placement of 4 stitches over 3 sharing a mesh. The stitches vary in length from 1 over 2 to 1 over 8. The step also varies from 1 to 2. Both step and stitch lengths are regulated by the expansion of the pattern from the corner niches where the stitches share a mesh.

After the center motif is worked, the pattern assumes a regular rhythm of 1 over 3 with a step of 1, with the exception of the corners where the stitches continue to share a mesh and to vary in length. The ripple of the pattern can be accentuated by contrasting colors.

53 KALEIDOSCOPE

Kaleidoscope uses repeats with corridors of long and short mosaic tiles to fit the repeats together.

Start in the center with 4 stitches each over 4 sharing a mesh. The first stitches are worked in a rhythm of 2 over 4 sharing a mesh, and extending 1 mesh beyond the existing center placement. Repeat in all 4 corners until a total of 5 complete rounds have been worked.

The spin-off for the repeat starts at the tip of the longest point where a stitch over 4 is added horizontally, sharing a mesh with the existing stitch.

The graph shows the filler corridor.

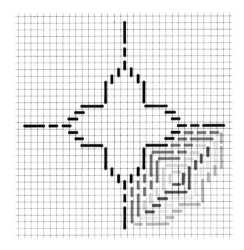

54 CLOISONNÉ

Particularly suitable for the tops of trinket boxes, Cloisonné effectively combines silk and metallic threads to achieve its jewel-like quality.

Worked on 14-mesh ecru canvas, the rhythm is 1 over 4 with a step of 1 down with the exception of compensation stitches occurring near intersections of lines. To establish pattern track, start at center top and work dark blue outline, followed by light blue outline. Connect points of dark blue line with orange to form 4 central boxes.

To fill inside boxes Work 2 rows of yellow. Fill with Diamond Eyelet Stitch.

To fill outside boxes Using gold metallic threads, work 9 Cross Stitches each over 2 sharing a center mesh to form a square. From the center stitch of each side of the square, work a long stitch to border, sharing a mesh at both ends of the stitch. Continue working metallic thread to shape "fans," using 4 stitches on either side of first long stitch. (Note that all stitches are worked into a single hole at base of fan.) Continental Stitches are used between fans—be sure they are worked in the same direction.

This design should be worked on a stretcher.

55 BAYADÈRE

This charming mosaic of building blocks is based on geometric forms like Sculptured Sticks (**20**). Its illusion change is particularly suitable for the close color transition that Bargello offers.

The pattern track is worked vertically 1 over 4 with a step of 1. The shelves of 4 stitches are repeated, interlocking with the adjoining shelf of stitches. In the voids left where the shelves don't meet, triangles are worked 1 over 7, over 5, over 3, over 1.

This pattern should be doodled or drawn in order to master the pattern track.

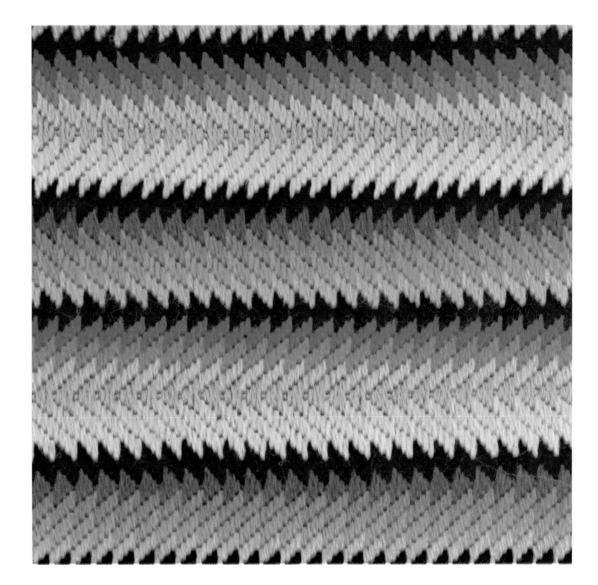

56 VICTORIA

From a paperweight comes this nostalgic Victorian pattern *for experts only* which is worked on 12-mesh Penelope canvas (the extra threads provide the meshes for the corridor stitches between the petals and square).

Two patterns are worked in unison: the 4-leaf clover and the secondary pattern that develops around the jeweled squares as the corridors are filled with brown wool.

Center the design in the middle of the canvas, working the 4 petals from the center out. As you work, separate all canvas threads by gently stabbing your needle between the meshes to separate them.

There are 8 stitches, each over 4 with a step of 1 to each of the 4 sides of the diamond-shaped petals. Work the petal outlines first, leaving a mesh void at the base. Shade their centers as the graph indicates from beige to tan. Each petal is worked in the same manner, starting from one side of the center-voided mesh and working outward.

Working from the side points of the diamond, move over 1 column leaving a void row and work a filled square of 8 stitches each side in Continental over 2, shading the colors from dark to light as you work toward the center. Be sure that all Continental Stitches slant in the same direction. There will be void corridors between these squares and the petals.

Turn the canvas back to the position the petals were worked from, and in the corridors left open between the petals and the squares, work a series of shared-mesh stitches using brown yarn. Start from the center of the side of the square and work horizontally and vertically, sharing a mesh in a rhythm of 1 over 9, over 8, over 7, over 5, over 4, over 3, over 2. The stitches form the frame for the petals and squares (see graph).

Border   The inside border is worked in a series of compensation stitches using velvet cording in the same rhythm as the adjacent worked areas. The outside border is worked in metallic thread in a rhythm of 1 over 4 and stitches are compensated where necessary.

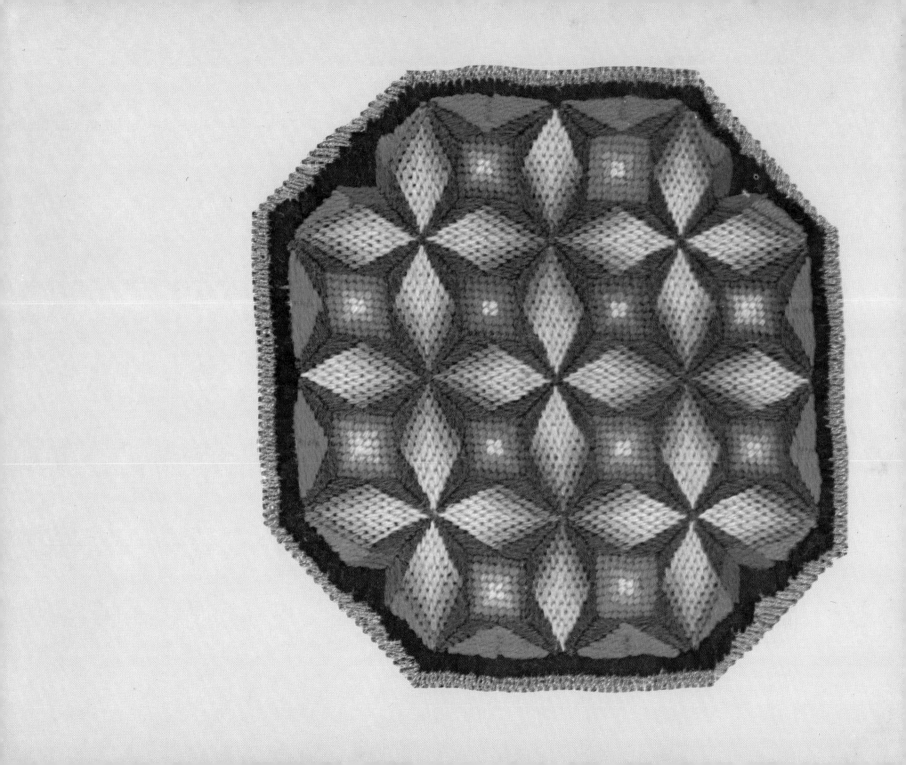

Almost any design can be copied in needlework
once you have become adept with its tools. Here a
piece of moiré ribbon was adapted for a free-form
needle painting worked in vertical Bargello
stitches against a Continental background.
(The illustration is turned on its side.)

Work out the pattern first on graph paper, then
transfer to canvas using indelible ink (see page
20 for technique).

Begin with metallic stitches, setting the pattern
rhythm with 2 rows of stitches worked vertically
over 2 and 3 threads. Step count is uneven to
produce the "watered" line characteristic of moiré
fabrics. Be sure that column widths are maintained
once established and that each color is used
consistently within columns.

The silk background is worked last in Continental.

TOP

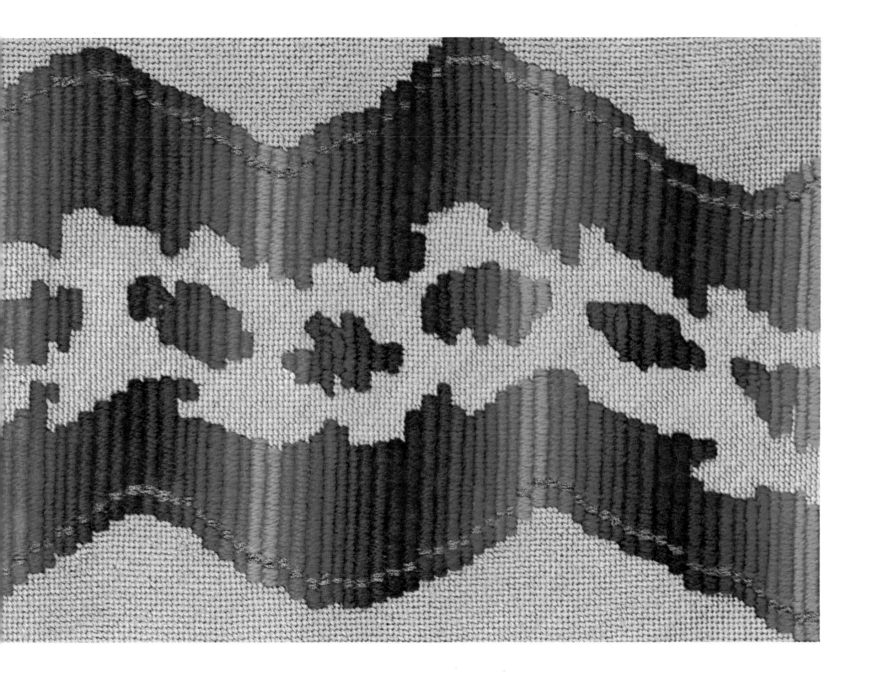

58 BARGELLO ROSE WITH COUCHED BORDER

In this elegant design featuring a couched border, French silk and wool combine with a metallic thread outline against a background of matte silk thread.

The border consists of antique gold braid laid on the canvas and couched at intervals with bright gold metallic thread. Measure couching braid carefully to make sure it is long enough to surround the perimeter of the design. Corners are continuations of couched border. End of braid is woven under starting point and covered with metallic thread.

Border rules are worked in bright gold thread in Continental on either side of the couched braid. *Work the border first.*

The rose is first outlined in the center of the canvas. (Part of the background has been left unworked to aid in tracing the outline.) Starting from the tip of the flower, work the outline in metallic threads. The rose is shaded from pink to red, the stitches worked vertically with a rhythm of 1 over 4, step 2.

The background is worked horizontally in Brick Stitch in the same rhythm as the rose.

This pattern should be worked on a stretcher.

Borders

Borders should be planned when beginning a pattern to coordinate with the central motif. They define compositions, accent the reciprocal relationships of color, and frame the completed result. Several periods may be mixed successfully by varying the borders and the central motif, and Bargello is an ideal medium for adapting these marginal areas to other types of needlework.

The subject of border design is worthy of a whole book and this section contains only a random sampling of ideas for motifs. It illustrates forms and shapes suitable for borders and will serve as a key to patterns in the Notebook that can be similarly adapted. Traditional motifs, Bargello Flame, groundings, chains and broken chains, geometric shapes, and fretwork patterns all lend themselves to border treatment.

Basically borders are formed by rhythmical arrangements of lines, dots, sections, angles, and divided or closed figures. Work with border motifs as segments as a framer does with mats, inserts, and shadow boxes. Top and bottom border patterns can be repeats or variations of a border theme, but side borders should be identical. Though they need not duplicate the top and bottom borders, they should be harmonious. The objective is a unified margin.

Borders frequently require combinations of stitches such as Bargello Flame with traméed "rules" to finish the margins or Basket Weave with Whipped Spider to fill corner medallions. Similarly, materials can be varied for effective design. Metallic threads duplicate the framer's gold leaf and silk will provide just the right highlight.

Always plot borders on graph paper before beginning on canvas. Thread count is intricate and you will need to follow a pattern developed especially for your design for proper placement of the border. Border widths vary, of course, but generally you should allow 2 inches on all 4 sides of the canvas for the border plus 2 inches around the outside for turn-under allowance. If the central motif is to be 14-inches square, you will need a piece of canvas 22-inches square.

Begin by locating and marking the centers of the horizontal and vertical sides of the canvas with threads or an indelible marking pen. From the marks, count off the number of threads needed to complete the central design. Outline this area with a marking pen. From your graph, determine the number of meshes needed for the border and draw the outside rule on canvas accordingly. If the corners are to be filled with squares, draw in boxes at corners; connect all corners of each box with bisecting lines—they will be used later for guidelines. If mitered corners are to be used, draw a diagonal line between the outside and inside corners.

Most border margins are outlined with a simple stitch of 1 over 2 to give the border a finished look. These stitches should be tramèed * to give dimension. Always work border rules first, whether using metallic, silk, or wool thread. This sets the outline and ensures that inside stitches will not encroach on the marginal areas. The rules should be sharply delineated.

Border patterns should be worked after you complete the central design, and starting points will vary according to the border pattern. If it has been carefully charted on a graph, the first stitch should not be a problem. Remember to work opposite sides in the same direction and sequence.

One problem in border design is adapting the pattern to

* That is, short vertical stitches are worked over long running stitches which serve as padding. Running stitches should be of uneven lengths to avoid ridges.

turn a corner. Corners can be worked to a square, mitered—that is, worked on a diagonal line—or worked in a continuous repeat. Working to a square is the simplest solution and can be used effectively with most borders. Mitered corners are modeled after the framer's technique of fitting right angles by means of a diagonal cut. Bargello Flame patterns are well suited for this treatment, and other motifs such as rope bands can be modified to intersect at corners. Corners worked in a continuous repeat are the most difficult, for they require exact fitting. Groundings, broken chain, and some fretwork patterns can be made into continuous repeat borders.

COMBINING BORDERS WITH PERIODS OF DECOR

A reciprocal relationship exists between certain periods of interior design and border motifs. The list below suggests borders suitable for various periods.

Oriental Basket Weave, bamboo, lattice, lotus leaf, Bargello Flame, and combinations of key and fretwork.

English Bargello Flame, laurel leaf, egg and dart, fretwork, linen fold, or arrow.

French Formal Chain and broken chain, grounding, geometric shapes, Bargello Flame, cording, couched or seeded sectors.

French Provincial Groundings, Bargello Flame, geometric shapes.

Early American Natural forms such as oak leaves, thistles, or most floral patterns, checkerboards, diaper groundings, solid bands, combinations of geometric shapes.

Colonial Williamsburg Bargello Flame, arrow.

Pennsylvania Dutch Natural forms of flowers, leaves, hearts, doodle stitchery, and hex signs.

Modern Fretwork patterns, chain and broken chain, groundings, Bargello Flame, doodle stitchery.

Traditional borders

Sources for border designs are unlimited. They can be suggested by familiar motifs found in the braids, ribbons, and bandings of contemporary chinaware, Oriental lattice work, fretwork patterns from Grecian vases, or Roman mosaics. Pictures from India offer ornamentation with a layered look, borders within borders, frame with mat.

ORIENTAL BASKET WEAVE

Basket Weave Stitches worked to a corner square make up this lovely border adapted from Oriental lacquerware. The corner square is filled with a Spider Stitch medallion centered in a field of Continental Stitches.

Start the basket weave at right of corner with a series of 7 stitches over 4 threads worked vertically from each of the border rules. Connect vertical blocks with a block of 5 stitches over 8 threads worked horizontally. Alternate this sequence with a block of 3 over 8 worked horizontally from each border rule, connected by a block of 7 over 8 worked vertically.

Caution: Stitches should be fairly loose to achieve woven effect; if tension is too great, canvas will not be covered.

Bargello Flame borders

Bargello patterns make beautiful frames if care is taken to control color so as not to overwhelm the central design. In the completed example on p. 143, strong color was used effectively to dramatize the dragon.

TORTOISE SHELL

Worked in silk and metallic threads, this pattern miters at the corner and its rhythm is disrupted without detracting from the design.

All metallic threads are worked first. The outside rules are tramèed in a rhythm of 1 over 2, and the gold miter at corners is tramèed on the bias, with covering stitches alternating 1 over 2, 1 over 1.

The inner Bargello pattern is 23-threads wide and is worked 1 over 4 with a step of 1 down. The colors are 6 tints and shades of yellow to brown in matte silk, 1 row of shiny yellow silk, 1 row of gold metallic thread. Start at inside rule, center pattern, and work toward outside. Note that side and bottom sequence are not uniform repeats.

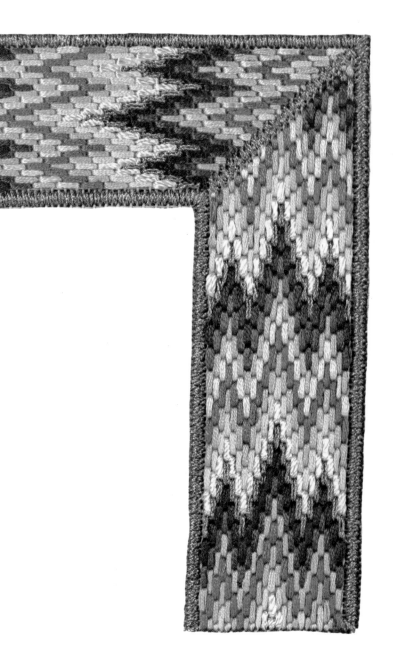

Grounding borders

Used as borders, these patterns are recessive and offer an opportunity to use 2 or more colors in a unified repeat.

TRELLIS

In this border, a continuous pattern weaves past the corner for a fine example of geometric unity. Trellis should be graphed to ensure accurate placement of corner repeats.

The outside rules are tramèed in mercerized cotton in a rhythm of 1 over 2. The inner border is 16-threads wide and is worked in a rhythm of 1 over 2 using tints and shades of orange wool with highlights of gold metallic and black 6-strand mercerized cotton. Shading from light to dark, start pattern at second complete row of 8 stitches to right of corner turn. Note that a compensation stitch over 1 is first stitch.

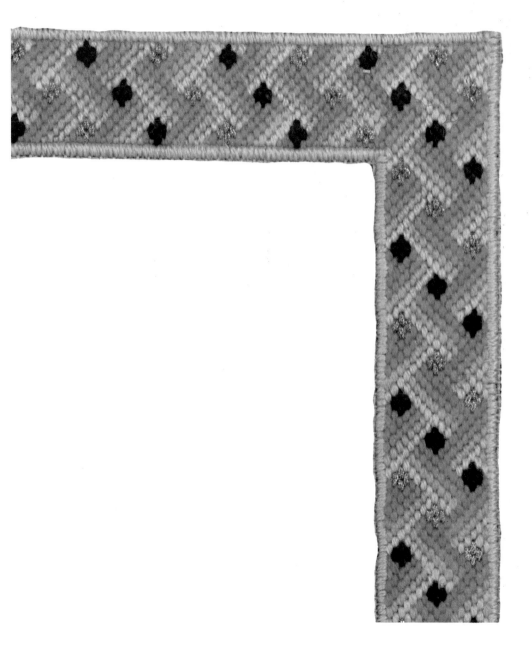

Chain borders

Chain and broken chain patterns are characterized by their interlaced, undulated, and rope bands. They are composed of circular, elliptical, square, or lozenge-shaped links and can be presented in profile or front view. Chain borders should be graphed, for repeats should match top and bottom and side to side. The following examples show continuous and mitered corner treatments.

BROKEN CHAIN

Starting from the corner, divide the repeats equally across the margins.

The outside rule is tramèed first in white wool in a rhythm of 1 over 2. Note there is no inside rule. The inner border is 20-threads wide and is worked in a rhythm of 1 over 4 with a step of 2, using yellow cotton thread and black wool. All stitches are in pairs. Count up 4 meshes from corner rule and work a black stitch over 4. This is the beginning of the first link of the broken chain. Follow your graph for the remainder of the repeat.

Fill background with Brick Stitch in white wool.

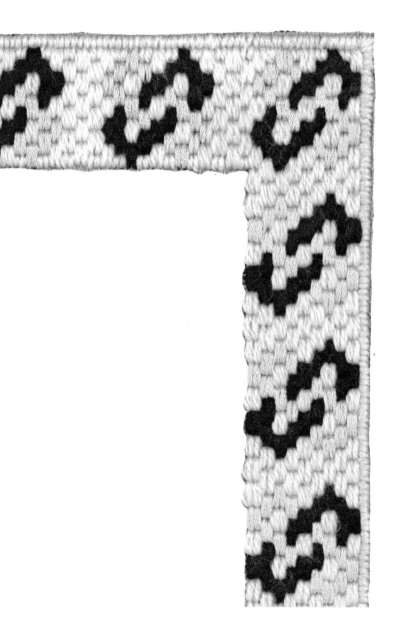

ROPE BORDER

Worked in 2 shades of blue with white wool, this border illustrates a continuous pattern that miters at the corner using stitches that share meshes. (Note that stitches used for mitering corners are of uneven lengths to compensate for turn.)

After planning on graph paper to ensure that rope is centered properly, mark off the border rules on the canvas and draw a slanted line on bias from corner to provide axis for turn. Work rules in Back Stitch using mercerized cotton; the rhythm is 1 over 2.

The rope rhythm varies from 1 over 6, 1 over 5, over 3, and over 2 with a step of 1. Start rope close to bias line and work toward corner, where compensation stitches complete the mitered turn. Check frequently and watch the accent areas to be certain their voids are equal. (Note that stitches are of uneven lengths around voids.)

Fill background with straight stitches.

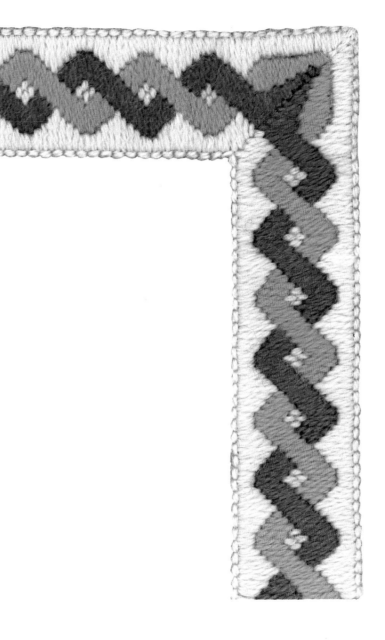

Geometric borders

Geometric shapes lend themselves well to borders and frames. They turn corners easily and give stability to a design.

FLORENTINE FRAME

Based on the Roman basilica—adapted to a polygon shape—this border has an inner mat that can be adjusted to fit larger or smaller motifs by increasing or decreasing the number of stitches on top and bottom in the same ratio.

The center frame is outlined in silk and accents the diamond form of the design. The bottom of the frame is only partially worked to aid in recognizing the repeat.

The inner border is worked in Pastilles (see graph on p. 90).

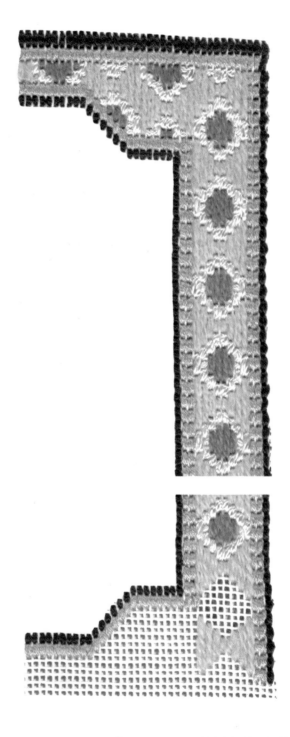

Miscellaneous borders

FEDERAL

This patriotic border features red, white, and blue and is ideally suited for side margins or can be worked on all 4 sides to corner squares if heavy accent is needed. The center band, 12-threads wide, is highlighted by a pyramid of white wool stitches over 8, 6, 4, and 2 worked against a filler background of dark blue wool. This unit is banded by groundings on either side worked in red wool with white accents. The outside rules are tramèed in blue silk in a rhythm of 1 over 2.

Continue outside and inside rules around canvas to frame central motif. Corners can be worked as squares and filled with a variation of Quilting Bee (**44**) in white wool.

STITCHKINS

Borders composed of freehand stitches can be used effectively to personalize your design. In this border children are playing ball, but activities of the matchstick figures can be developed in numerous ways.

Stitchkins is planned for a width of 16 threads, including 3 rows of outline stitches worked in Continental. The figures are stitched over 1, over 2, or over 3, and threads should be left a little loose to give depth to the figures. The background has been left unfinished to aid in counting the threads. It should be worked in white wool in Continental.

Graph your design first, dividing the figures equally across the length of the border. Activities can continue around the border but remember to position side motifs in a vertical stance.

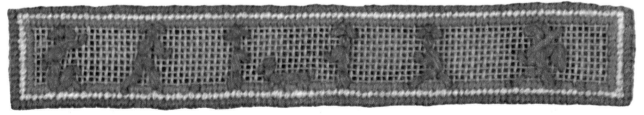

BARGELLO BORDER WITH NEEDLEPOINT DRAGON

Reciprocal forms of fangs and claws are repeated in the color-coordinated Bargello border worked to a mitered corner. The border is worked from the center of each side using a rhythm of 1 over 6 and 2 over 2 in shades of apricot, blue, and green wool. Each color group is separated by a band of ecru cotton.

The mitered corner is worked to a diagonal line with the pattern repeat continuous from the outside of border edge to the inside line where it compensates. Repeat this border on all 4 sides, watching the direction of stitches so that opposite borders match.

An inner frame of 1 row of ecru cotton worked in Continental borders the notched edge worked in navy blue, also using Continental. To achieve the notched edge and keep the blue from showing through the light background, work 1 Continental Stitch, another in the row above, and 1 adjoining the first stitch; repeat this sequence. The open mesh is filled with ecru cotton.

Outer edge is worked in Continental using 4 tints and shades of blue wool.

The dragon is worked in Continental using metallic, silk, and wool against a background of silk and wool in wave pattern using closely related tints of blue.

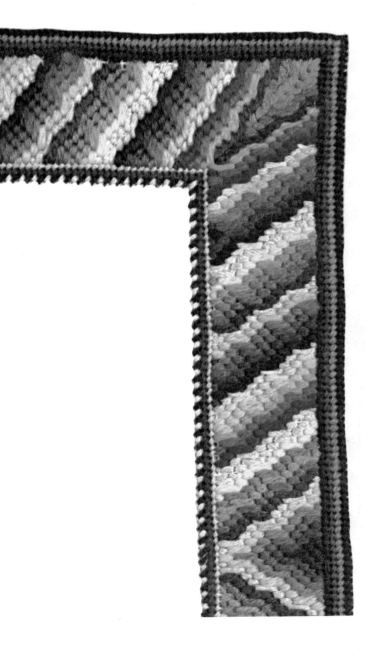

Sources
of information

Bibliography

In compiling this list, we have selected books that are interesting and valuable which deal, at least in part, with topics not covered or not fully covered in this volume. Generally we are including books from our libraries that we have found useful. This method of selection is highly subjective, of course, and the omission of any particular book does not necessarily indicate disagreement or disapproval on our part.

The list is divided by subject, but many titles contain material on subjects other than those under which they are listed. Those that cover all or most aspects of specific types of needlework are divided into stitch classifications. The second section is devoted to books on design and its application to needlework, and the last, "Miscellaneous," contains books *about* needlework rather than on how to do it.

BARGELLO STITCHERY

Bargello and Related Stitchery, by Charles Barnes and David P. Blake. Hearthside Press, New York, 1971, 245 pp. Excellent sourcebook for Bargello stitches with easy-to-follow diagrams; includes complete instructions for making a number of outstanding boutique items.

Florentine Embroidery, by Barbara Snook. Charles Scribner's Sons, New York, 1967, 160 pp. Excellent graphs and pattern classifications.

CANVAS AND CREWEL STITCHERY

American Crewelwork, by Mary Taylor Landon and Susan Burrows Swan. The Macmillan Company, New York, 1970, 192 pp. A description of crewelwork stitches with designs showing how these stitches are used. Study of antique American needlework with suggestions for modern adaptations.

The Art of Crewel Embroidery, by Mildred J. Davis. Crown Publishers, Inc., New York, 1962, 224 pp. The many lovely designs illustrated in this book, with easy-to-follow directions, will help the embroiderer to expand her ability in design, color, and stitchery.

Canvas Embroidery, by Hebe Cox. Mills & Boon, Ltd., London, 1960, 91 pp. Comprehensive booklet with practical suggestions on how to make your own designs and on materials to be used. Clear diagrams of stitches.

Crewel Embroidery, by Erica Wilson. Charles Scribner's Sons, New York, 1962, 154 pp. Features creative use of stitches with outstanding stitch techniques.

Mary Thomas's Dictionary on Embroidery Stitches. Hodder and Stoughton, London, 1934, 244 pp. More than 300 stitches are illustrated with precise diagrams in this classic book of stitches.

Needlepoint, by Hope Hanley. Charles Scribner's Sons, New York, 1964, 160 pp. Illustrated instructions for over 50 canvas stitches. Excellent for techniques of finishing and mounting your own needlework.

100 Embroidery Stitches (pamphlet). Coats Sewing Group, Glasgow, Scotland, 1967, 48 pp. Comprehensive list of embroidery stitches with diagrams, grouped into families according to their structure.

The Stitches of Creative Embroidery, by Jacqueline Enthoven. Reinhold Publishing Company, New York, 1964, 212 pp. Informative and very interesting book for readers doing crewelwork. Clear description of creative stitches with easy-to-follow diagrams.

NEEDLEWORK DESIGN

Bargello by Elsa S. Williams. Van Nostrand Reinhold Company, New York, 1967, 64 pp. Superb designs for Bargello.

Do-It-All-Yourself Needlepoint, by Joan Scobey and Lee Parr McGrath. Simon and Schuster, New York, 1971, 184 pp. Comprehensive instructions for designing canvas from start to finish. Outstanding boutique and assembling instructions.

Ecclesiastical Embroidery, by Beryl Dean. B.T. Batsford, Ltd., London, 1958, 258 pp. Discusses basic principles of design, suitable materials, and has excellent chapter on symbolism.

Embroideries and Fabrics for Synagogue and Home. Hearthside Press, New York, 1966, 224 pp. Five thousand years of ornamental needlework are discussed.

Needlepoint by Design, by Maggie Lane. Charles Scribner's Sons, New York, 1970, 114 pp. Variations on Chinese themes graphed and explained; particularly useful for planning and working borders.

Needlepoint Design, by Louis Gartner, Jr. William Morrow and Company, New York, 1970, 192 pp. Covers a wide range of projects including rugs, slippers, and wall hangings. Exceptional for shading and shadow-play techniques in Needlepoint design.

GENERAL DESIGN

Creative Color, by Faber Bierren. Reinhold Publishing Company, New York, 1961. Scientific theories of color presented simply and imaginatively.

A Grammar of Chinese Lattice, by Daniel Dye. Harvard University Press, Cambridge, 1949. With more than 500 line drawings this is a treasure house of motifs.

Handbook of Plant and Floral Ornament from Early Herbals, by Richard G. Hatton. Dover Publications, Inc., New York, 1960, 539 pp. Twelve hundred illustrations selected from herbals, woodcuts, or copper-plate engravings arranged for decorative usage.

Monograms and Ciphers, by A.A. Turbayne. Dover Publications, Inc., New York, 1968. Shows how to design with letters; over 1,200 designs.

The Principles of Harmony and Contrast of Color, by M.E. Chevreul. Van Nostrand Reinhold Company, New York, 1967. The explanatory notes by Faber Bierren make clear the original concept of color harmonies.

The Styles of Ornament, by Alexander Speltz. Dover Publications, Inc., New York, 1959, 647 pp. More than 3,000 illustrations; 400 are full-page plates showing motifs of ornament according to historical periods.

Weaving and Needlecraft Color Course, by William and Doris Justema. Van Nostrand Reinhold Company, New York, 1971, 160 pp. A unique color guide especially designed for those who work with weaving and needlework threads.

MISCELLANEOUS

American Needlework, by Georgiane Brown Harbeson. Crown Publishers, Inc., 1938, 221 pp. This book describes the origins and gives the history of decorative stitchery and embroidery from the late sixteenth century to the twentieth century. A very practical handbook with a selection of delightful works from each period.

English Domestic Needlework, by Therle Hughes. The Macmillan Company, New York, 1961, 255 pp. History and examples of museum needlework for reference.

Needlepoint in America, by Hope Hanley. Charles Scribner's Sons, New York, 1969, 160 pp. Traces the history of American Needlepoint and Needlepoint design. Old stitches are revived.

A Pictorial History of Embroidery, by Marie Schuette and Sigrid Muller-Christensen. Frederick A. Praeger, New York, 1964, 336 pp. Illustrates museum pieces and embroideries in private collections covering works from third to fourth centuries to the twentieth century. A unique source of inspiration for creative embroiderers.

Organizations

The Embroiderers' Guild of America, Inc. is an educational, non-profit organization, founded in 1958. For 12 years it was affiliated with the Embroiderers' Guild of London. Its purpose is to set and maintain high standards of design, color, and workmanship in all kinds of embroidery and canvas work. Toward this end, the Guild serves as an information source for individual needlewomen throughout the United States. The Guild also provides portfolios which include photographs and specimens of needlework and slides. It publishes a quarterly, *Needle Arts,* and has designs and pamphlets for sale. Write to 120 E. 56th Street, New York, N.Y. 10022.

Suppliers

With the revival of interest in needlework, the production of wool yarns and silk and metallic threads has been increasing in recent years. Precious silk and metallic threads, once found only in Europe, can be located in department stores and needlework shops across the United States. In addition, exciting new materials from synthetic fibers are being introduced and these can be substituted for the more expensive yarns and threads. If materials are not available in your area, the following manufacturers or suppliers will suggest retail outlets for you to contact.

C.M. Almy & Sons, Inc.
gold and silver metallic thread
37 Purchase Street
New York, New York 10580

Brunswick Worsted Mills, Inc.
wool, orlon, mohair, angora yarns; canvas
230 Fifth Avenue
New York, New York 10001

Columbia-Minerva
yarn and canvas
295 Fifth Avenue
New York, New York 10010

C.R. Meissner Company
silk thread, Colbert wool, French Toile Colbert
22 East 29th Street
New York, New York 10016

The D.M.C. Corporation
Retors à Broder, Moulinè, and cotton perle,
gold and silver metallic thread, canvas
107 Trumbull Street
Elizabeth, New Jersey 07206

Handwork Tapestries
French Toile Colbert and penelope canvas;
all supplies for needlework canvas
81 North Forest Avenue
Rockville Centre, New York

Joan Toggitt, Ltd.
Marlitt and Bella Donna rayon thread, Pearsall silks,
Knox's linen thread, canvas, wools, D.M.C. threads
1170 Broadway, Suite 406
New York, New York 10001

Needlecraft House
yarns, canvas, needles
West Townsend, Massachusetts 01474

Paternayan Bros., Inc.
Persian yarns; crewel, tapestry, and knitting yarns;
needlepoint canvases; monk's cloth
312 East 95th Street
New York, New York 10028

Tinsel Trading Co.
gold and silver Lamé thread
47 West 38th Street
New York, New York

Directory of art needlework shops

There are many excellent needlework shops throughout the United States. Below is a brief list of stores that will provide you with the raw materials for designing your own patterns if you do not have a favorite shop nearby.

CALIFORNIA

The Needlecraft Shop
4501 Van Nuys Boulevard
Sherman Oaks, California 91403

CONNECTICUT

The Hook 'N' Needle
1869 East State Street
Westport, Connecticut 06880

DISTRICT OF COLUMBIA

The Elegant Needle
5430 MacArthur Boulevard, N.W.
Washington, D.C. 20016

The Woolgatherer
1608 20th Street, N.W.
Washington, D.C. 20009

FLORIDA

Yarn and Design Studio
2156 Ponce de Leon Boulevard
Coral Gables, Florida 33134

GEORGIA

The Snail's Pace, Inc.
548 East Paces Ferry Road, N.E.
Atlanta, Georgia 30305

MASSACHUSETTS

The Crafts Centre
Quaker Road
Nantucket, Massachusetts 02554

The Stitchery
Wellesley Hills, Massachusetts 02181

MICHIGAN

The Sampler
1011 S. Washington
Royal Oak, Michigan 48067

MINNESOTA

Stitch Niche
2866 Hennepin Avenue
Minneapolis, Minnesota 55408

MISSISSIPPI

Pandora's Box
P.O. Box E
Merigold, Mississippi 38759

NEW JERSEY

Crafty Women
Colts Town Shoppes
Highway 34
Colts Neck, New Jersey 07722

Janet's
Highway 35
Sea Girt, New Jersey 08750

NEW YORK

The Open Door to Stitchery
4 Bond Street
Great Neck, New York 11021

Alice Maynard
558 Madison Avenue
New York, New York 10022

Boutique Margot
26 West 54th Street
New York, New York 10019

NORTH CAROLINA

Ruth Leary's
382 North Elm Street
Greensboro, North Carolina 27401

OKLAHOMA

The Yarn Garden, Inc.
10956 North May Avenue
Oklahoma City, Oklahoma 73120

PENNSYLVANIA

Creative Stitchery
2116 Walnut Street
Philadelphia, Pennsylvania 19103

TEXAS

Deux Amis, Inc.
3708 Crawford
Austin, Texas 78731

VIRGINIA

Laura Weaver Needlework
Hotel Patrick Henry
617 South Jefferson Street
Roanoke, Virginia 24011

WASHINGTON

Phalice's Thread Web
West 1301 14th Avenue
Spokane, Washington 99204

Index